"We have filled our homes with stuff, our calendars with activities, and our hearts with a desire for more. Keri Wyatt Kent's GODSPACE invites us to declutter our hearts, our homes, and our calendars in order to make room for the inconvenient wonder of God's presence. Kent tells stories from her own life and offers practical suggestions on how we can open ourselves up to God's work in our homes, our communities, and the world. With humor, insight, and concrete examples, Keri Wyatt Kent has written a book that encourages me to make meaningful changes that will enable less space for disappointment and more space for God."

—Amy Julia Becker, author of *A Good and Perfect Gift* and *Small Talk*

"GODSPACE is at once deeply spiritual and handily practical. Through personal stories, biblical application, and tried-and-true wisdom, Keri Wyatt Kent's book opens our hearts and minds to make space for God in the everyday."

—Caryn Rivadeneira, author of *Grit and Grace: Heroic Women of the Bible* and *Broke: What Financial Desperation Revealed about God's Abundance*

"GODSPACE is destined to become a spiritual classic, one of those books I keep on my shelf to reread and review whenever I need a spiritual boost. It is both inspirational and practical, encouraging and challenging. From the very beginning, Keri Wyatt Kent sets out to help the reader see "everyday life soaked with the presence of God." She then demonstrates practical applications of spiritual disciplines in lovely, whimsical ways. A great book to study with others or give to anyone who yearns to feel the presence of God."

—Dale Hanson Bourke, author

"In a noisy, distracted culture, the word *mindfulness* frequently gets thrown around as a remedy for anxiety and disconnection. But what does it mean to be mindful? In her new book, Keri Wyatt Kent does much more than promote a more mindful way of living. She details seven specific spiritual practices—including critical thinking—that give us the chance to slow down, become more aware of the gifts and grace around us, and draw closer to the Divine. This is a beautiful, intelligent book—a gift!"

—Jennifer Grant, author of *Wholehearted Living,*
*Love You More,* and *When Did Everybody*
*Else Get So Old?*

# GODSPACE

## BOOKS BY KERI WYATT KENT

*Deeply Loved: 40 Ways in 40 Days to Experience the
Heart of Jesus*

*Deeper into the Word: Old Testament*

*Deeper into the Word: New Testament*

*Simple Compassion: Devotions to Make a Difference in Your
Neighborhood and Your World*

*Rest: Living in Sabbath Simplicity*

*Oxygen: Deep Breathing for the Soul*

*Listen: Finding God in the Story of Your Life*

*Breathe: Creating Space for God in a Hectic Life*

*The Garden of the Soul*

*God's Whisper in a Mother's Chaos*

# GODSPACE

## EMBRACING THE INCONVENIENT ADVENTURE OF INTIMACY WITH GOD

## KERI WYATT KENT

New York   Nashville

FaithWords
Hachette Book Group
1290 Avenue of the Americas, New York, NY 10104
faithwords.com
twitter.com/faithwords

First edition: September 2017

FaithWords is a division of Hachette Book Group, Inc.
The FaithWords name and logo are trademarks of Hachette Book Group, Inc.

The publisher is not responsible for websites (or their content) that are not owned by the publisher.

Library of Congress Control Number: 2017941991

ISBNs: 978-1-4789-7071-2 (trade paperback), 978-1-4789-7072-9 (ebook)

Printed in the United States of America

LSC-C

10  9  8  7  6  5  4  3  2

*For Melanie & Aaron*

# Contents

# In Our Crowded Life, Where Does God Fit?

Where is the space for God?

Spiritual disciplines like prayer, study, and solitude have been recommended as ways to connect with God, dive deeper spiritually, grow in faith. These practices would be great, if we had the time, right?

When I first came back to church, after a brief but spectacularly unsatisfying year or two of postcollege wandering, I wanted a deep spiritual life. God hungry, I craved more than an obligatory "daily quiet time" could provide. I chafed under the odd legalism of evangelical subculture, longed for a richer experience of faith, a way to embrace mystery and contemplation. Finding myself at a large church, I joined a small group where we read and discussed both Dallas Willard's *The Spirit of the Disciplines* and Richard Foster's *Celebration of Discipline*, comparing them side by side. I was kind of the wild child of the group, but I felt loved and accepted. We talked about practices like solitude, prayer, fasting, and so on. I loved and needed both the community of the group and these disciplines. I eagerly scheduled days at Catholic retreat centers, dabbled with fasting (until the night I passed out at church from not eating all day), and even began writing books about spiritual practices. Exploring deeper spirituality, ancient paths rediscovered, spiritual transformation, and contemplation fed my soul.

Such ancient practices can connect us to God, enliven our souls. But it's been said that the trouble with finding a way to God is that we grow to love the way more than we love God. Our practices can help, or hinder. My own spiritual practices drew me closer to God, yet tempted me to pride. I could easily feel quietly superior to those who didn't practice their faith in the same way I did. My delight in discovering a more contemplative faith had a shadow side, which looked down on those who had not yet explored what I considered to be a better way to relate to God. I'd become just a little judge-y sometimes, which threatened to undo all the ways in which I had grown deeper. A day at the monastery fed my soul. My pride, however, unwittingly starved it. Thankfully, leaning into these practices offers a gentle self-correction. When I got quiet, I'd become painfully aware of my own judgmental attitude, mourn my own pride, realize how far I had to go.

And any spiritual practices can only help if we have time for them. If we try to squeeze in some solitude, shoehorn in a bit of contemplation, pack an extra prayer into a life already crammed too full, those life-giving disciplines deflate, lose their potential power. We might be very religious about prayer or study, but are those practices actually helping us grow, connect with God, change to become Christ-like? Practices can be wonderful, but if they're part of an overcrowded, too-busy life, they are more likely to veer into the ditch of legalism, or feel like a burden.

They can become a source of pride. We can make them an attempt to earn God's favor—even though we may not dare say that out loud or even admit that motive to ourselves. They can become yet another obligation in our overcommitted lives. Their meaning can leach out over time, leaving empty rituals where connection once flourished. I know this because I've made these mistakes.

I've also found that traditional practices can be compartmentalized. You can get really good at the practices, but they can feel disconnected from your real life—you know, the life where you squabble with your husband and nag your kids and are running late for work again, and the life where you sit on the front porch with your friends, have a beer, and talk about stuff—like how your marriage is actually doing, how parenting teenagers is genuinely hard, why you think you might quit your job, or how someone you thought was a friend let you down. Solitude, silence, study, prayer, even fasting, all have their place. But it's easy to do these things and then go back to real life. The life where you are yourself, for better or worse. Spirituality, disembodied from both our struggles and our joys, will likely whither.

After years as a spiritual-formation writer and speaker, I realized that what has formed my spirit the most is not how often I get away for a solitude retreat but what I do when I get home. My daily life—how I respond to my neighbors and my family—is just as formational, and sometimes harder, than spending time in solitude or prayer.

The way I found God space—sacred moments in which we encounter the holy—was to begin to see all of my life as lived in the space of God.

Finding God space is like trying to put more air into your life. Air is all around you, but you don't notice it. Just as you may not think about air, you can ignore God if you are moving too fast, rushing around distracted. By slowing down, you can begin to see that everyday life is soaked with the presence of God. You can see God if only you reframe your life a bit. If you stop, breathe, and live your faith, you engage in what some call an embodied spirituality. The term *embodied spirituality*, like many other terms that belonged in ancient days to Christianity, has been co-opted by other traditions—including Paganism and New Age. My goal is to reclaim for Jesus followers this accurate descriptor of living faith, to remind us that it was a Christian term to begin with.

Our faith is not just what we think, or even believe. It's not a list of our philosophical oppositions, although to listen to some Christians, you might mistakenly draw that conclusion. Our soul, housed in our body, is transformed in part by our actions and practices, what we do with our body. Simply slowing down is done with your body.

As the Bible says, "Faith without works is dead" (James 2:20 KJV). We make our faith a reality by what we do. Whether that's opening our home to someone as we practice hospitality, or taking the time to rest on Sabbath, we don't just contemplate it, we take bodily action.

As Dallas Willard explains, "The secret of the standard, historically proven spiritual disciplines is precisely that they *do* respect and count on the bodily nature of human personality. They all deeply and essentially involve bodily conditions and activities. Thus they show us effectively *how* we can 'offer our bodies as living sacrifices, holy and acceptable unto God' and how our 'spiritual worship' (Rom. 12:1) really is inseparable from the offering up of our bodies in specific physical ways."[1]

Willard also notes, "The human body *is* the focal point of human existence. Jesus had one. We have one. Without the body in its proper place, the pieces of the puzzle of new life in Christ do not realistically fit together, and the idea of *really* following him and becoming like him remains a practical impossibility."[2]

If your goal is only to get really good at spiritual practices, or if you're reading this because you think you should or ought to, I suggest you revise that goal. This book is an invitation to live in grace—with your whole self. Actions that genuinely create space for God are not motivated by legalism or an attempt to earn God's favor. They're a response to a winsome invitation, a way of diving deeper into the adventure of intimacy with God.

Spiritual practices, which Christians have engaged in for centuries, are not something we do in order to get good at doing them. The aim of prayer, for example, is not to be excellent at praying, but to draw closer to God. The goal is not impressing God, or anyone else, but intimate communion with God. If our objective in prayer is to get good at anything, it would be to get really skilled at listening to God, to live more fully aware of grace. We pray not for our own sake, but for the sake of others. Prayer tunes our ear to the divine whisper, not so that we might brag of our spiritual depth, but so that we would hear and obey God. The invitation: to love others out of the overflow of God's love for us, made known to us by the communion we experience when we truly listen, instead of merely talk.

In the same way, other practices form us into people who love our neighbors and love God—Christ-like people—rather than people who are experts at religious activities. If we should desire to make progress in anything, it should be advancement toward Christ-likeness. We tend to act like the people we hang around with, so intimacy and connection with Jesus will begin to transform our actions and our thoughts. These practices will offer God room to work in your life, to transform you into a person who looks and acts more like Jesus. Practices do not earn God's favor or meet any divine requirement. Practices are simply ways to respond to the grace, the unmerited favor, we have already received.

## "I'm So Busy!"

We can get very busy for God, rush past opportunities for intimacy. Our default answer to the casual "How are you?" is the descriptor for life in the twenty-first century: "So busy!" We say we're busy because we equate it with significance. We feel busy even when we are not. The stress of handling onslaughts of information, decisions, images, and words assails us. We're busy and, as a result, weary. We long for rest, for margin, for space. God longs for that space as well, longing to fill it with presence, intimacy, joy, grace.

We say we have no time, but perhaps it would be more accurate to say we're distracted. We think we don't have a moment but find time to update the world on the details of our day via social media or binge-watch television. I know this from experience. I'll log on to Facebook just to check and then realize an hour later that I am simply surfing through updates from people I don't actually know in real life, or watching videos of dogs, horses, or little kids who can sing like Pavarotti. (I'm not a cat person, sorry. Otherwise cat videos would be in this list.)

Hurry taints even our spirituality. A franticness keeps us at the surface and doesn't let us rest in God's presence. We rush through prayer. We add another church activity to our crammed schedules. We faithfully read our Bible but forget what we've read a moment later. Our faith can feel disconnected, hollow.

To our weary souls, God offers the Sabbath. Wrapped in the words of commandment and law, we may not recognize it for what it is: a gift. The only way to unwrap it is to practice it. When we do so—not perfectly, not legalistically, but expectantly and humbly—we receive the gift, the grace, of time. We all are given seven days in a week. What we do with those days can allow us to see God and experience the divine, or not.

What if the ancient practice of Sabbath—a day to set aside work and focus on God—could be the gateway to other practices that impact our pace of life, our experience of God's grace, our awareness of God's presence? What if taking a day off actually made us more patient, gentle, more aware of the needs of others?

What if other spiritual disciplines, flowing out of Sabbath, could also open up space for God? What if slowing our pace allowed us to enjoy God in new ways, through practices we might never have considered? What if loving our neighbor begins with slowing down enough to actually notice our neighbor? What if our daily lives could be interwoven with practices we didn't have to go to the monastery to engage in?

If we slow down a bit, we might have time to consider the questions: What does the pace of my life have to do with the health of my soul? How does the health of my soul impact the people around me, the people I'm trying to love: spouse, neighbors, kids?

We sometimes define faith as intellectual assent to certain truths. We argue about ideas, judge who is in and out based on philosophical or political positions. While right belief is essential, it is not the whole story. Orthopraxy (right practice) is just as important as orthodoxy (right doctrine). Our contemplation should lead to action. Our faith, to practice. Our knowledge about God, to deep communion with God. We do not always live in this truth.

We say that everything is spiritual, yet we actually believe certain things are more spiritual: praying parroted words, eyes shut and hands folded; dutifully filling in the blanks in our Bible study workbook; wondering what we're doing wrong when the right way to connect with God doesn't quite work for us anymore.

We need some new ways to commune deeply with God. That means we must create space for God, find God space in our busy lives.

Deep communion with God won't happen by squeezing God into a life full to bursting with busyness. A life full of obligations and stress, that has no margin, no time, won't accommodate God space.

What if the way to find "God space"—open space for God in our lives, schedules, hearts—was to live at "God's pace"?

What if adjusting the pace of our lives to God's sacred rhythms could help us find God space—sacred moments in which we encounter the holy? What if the presence of God we seek is right there, but we miss it when we move to the demands of the culture instead of to God's gentle invitation?

Practice, not perfection, is the path to orthopraxy. We engage in ways of living that usher us into God space at God's pace. The practices in this book all invite us to live out our faith, to live and act in ways that reflect the grace of Sabbath, a pace that is unhurried yet deliberate and productive. We can learn to travel at God's pace via practices that seem unrelated to time: worship, hospitality, generosity. For these things cannot be done in a hurry. By their very nature, these practices, both new and ancient, invite us to slow down, to quiet our restless hearts, to rest in God's goodness where we begin to change.

## Practices Bring Alignment

A year ago, my then-twenty-one-year-old daughter wrote me a birthday letter. Our family joke is that my love language consists of mushy letters in which my husband or children write or speak words of affirmation. It took years of training to get my husband to embrace this. One of our birthday traditions when the kids were growing up was to go around the dinner table and tell something we liked about the birthday person.

This birthday, a hoped-for visit had been delayed and my daughter was not at my table, but in California at college. She wrote a note that said, "I'm sorry you couldn't be in California for your b-day. Instead of writing you a mushy letter, I decided to compile a list of values that I am grateful you raised me with…"

She then listed thirteen random values beginning with "hospitality, gathering people around the table," and moving on to "Sabbath Sundays, quiet time," and some I didn't expect, like "very limited television" and "chores, pitching in." Her list also included "caring for the poor" and "simple living." And also, "learning from my own mistakes" and "letting me be my own person."

The letter is a treasure; I have it hanging on the wall by my desk, because, yes, those are all values I raised her to embrace. I sometimes wondered whether those values would stick, but for the most part they have. I also want it there to remind me to keep on living according to those values, engaging in those practices.

To teach those values, we didn't just talk about them. We practiced them. We embodied them. We practiced Sabbath, we practiced letting the kids learn from their mistakes, we practiced hospitality. It was not always easy.

Nothing compares to a child as a mirror of your life. From the time they first speak and you cringe to hear them mimicking your not-so-pretty words and tone of voice, to the teen years where they push so hard against boundaries you set, to young adulthood where they begin, you hope, to live according to what you taught, they reflect you.

My daughter's letter, and countless other conversations, got me thinking about spiritual practice, and how we impart values to our children, how we reinforce those values in ourselves. Does our ideology align with our actual life? Practices are what bring about that alignment—slowly, over time. So when I thought about practices that have formed me and my family spiritually, ones I wanted to offer to you, my reader, I started with my daughter's list.

## Listening to Your Life

Parker Palmer once wrote, "Before you tell your life what you intend to do with it, listen for what it intends to do with you. Before you tell your life what truths and values you have decided to live up to, let your life tell you what truths you embody, what values you represent."[3]

If I listen to my life, I come to an inconvenient and uncomfortable truth: I'm often more comfortable with people outside the church than in it. I'm a strong feminist. I love Jesus but I don't fit the "church lady" mold. I'm an 8 on the Enneagram, which means I can be difficult, opinionated, strong-willed. Nicknamed "the challenger," 8s are, according to one summary, "self-confident, decisive, willful, and confrontational." That's a pretty accurate description of me, which, in the church, would be more acceptable if I were a dude. But I'm not.

I tried for a long time to be the contemplative, deep, spiritual formation gal. I wasn't inauthentic; I found it life-giving, and it balanced out the side of me that is a bit tightly wound. Because I'm by nature opinionated and assertive, I questioned my own ability to be contemplative and deep. Could I be both? I almost gave up on the whole contemplative thing, but I realized that while the contemplative practices are helpful and necessary, I also had to figure out how to balance those with practices that engage my daily life.

Solitude and silence, prayer and contemplation—these are helpful, yet not the only way to grow in Christ-likeness. When I loved the not-so-lovable (that sometimes included my immediate family) that was a spiritual practice. When I chose to be generous, even if I didn't feel like it, it formed my soul. When I offered a cup of cold water or a meal to strangers, or to my own children, I was not just obeying Jesus but becoming more like him. In other words, practices that are merely part of my daily living had just as much potential impact on spiritual growth as activities I'd elevated to be more spiritually significant. Sharing a meal can be as formational as prayer—if you approach it as such.

*GodSpace* offers you an opportunity to play with untraditional spiritual practices, new disciplines, and consider the possibility that God could meet you in unexpected ways.

This book will explore seven practices that individuals, groups, and even families can do to live at God's pace, in order to create some God space. These seven don't comprise an exhaustive list. They're some I've found helpful as I've tried for more than two decades to intentionally live in what I call Sabbath Simplicity. I don't have it all figured out. I've made a lot of mistakes, but I've tried to learn from those mistakes. I hope by telling you my story, you will be encouraged, guided, or at least know you're not the only one desperate for a little margin.

A simpler, saner life is possible. This book will help you move toward it without having to go to a monastery. I'm inviting you to a lifestyle, not offering a religious to-do list. The first practice, Sabbath, informs all the others. All are interconnected, are part of a theology of Sabbath, a way of unpacking the grace and gift of Sabbath time.

Join me on the journey to find some God space, by living at God's pace.

# Sabbath

## *Space in My Calendar*

Fire, fierce and warming, glows in the worn brick fireplace. The washing machine swishes steady in the background.

Sabbath is over, but glows like an ember in the early darkness of an autumn evening.

Sabbath crept in unannounced at sundown Saturday, as we had dinner with friends at their home. I'd served those friends by watching their kids for the afternoon. So Sabbath began with a meal around a table with friends. Conversation with kids and adults was peppered with moments of tender conversation, and moments of wiping up spilled Gatorade. After dinner, the dads and kids played Wii bowling.

Sunday morning my son left early to meet his small group leader for breakfast before church, my daughter went to lead her small group in the three-year-old room at church, and my husband and I went to church. We went in different directions, but all experienced community. Thanks to texting, we kept in touch through the day.

After church I came home and lounged on the couch, reading. My daughter read and napped upstairs. My son sent a text that he was going out to lunch with friends. I read an article about walking in the woods. Inspired, I went for a walk in the woods, enjoying a cool but sunny fall afternoon. Milkweed loosed its hold on fluffy contents, ancient pear trees in a meadow held their fruit even though their leaves had already fallen. Sabbath is an open day, when there is nothing else I have to do. It makes you walk differently, more attentive and less driven.

I came home, puttered a bit in the garden, let myself be sun-kissed and dirt-stained. I cannot think of a more perfect day than one I can spend outside playing in the garden. I divided perennials, snipped and trimmed a few branches. Breathed in fall air, talked with and listened to Jesus.

Later, I cooked—a creative enterprise that never feels like work to me. My daughter and I snacked on the roasted carrots and parsnips as soon as I pulled them from the oven, and she took notes on how I make my pork chops with apples and onions.

"I'm glad you're a good cook," she said.

"I'm glad you're not a picky eater," I replied.

"I think those two might be related."

We talked about college applications, which led to a conversation on our Myers-Briggs profiles. Which I had plenty of time for, because I didn't need to go anywhere, do anything. I was fully present, discussing the introvert-extrovert question, as we ate veggies straight off the baking sheet. We got too full from eating all the carrots to even want the dinner, so I left it on the stove until my son came home from playing volleyball.

Sabbath is a day when I am never too busy to do what I am doing. Where structure is released, have-tos banished.

I don't force my kids to "do" Sabbath with me (I'm glad they go to church at this stage of the game), but they know that on Sunday, they can find me, and that I am imminently interruptible. That availability is part of my Sabbath practice, and one they count on.

Around dinnertime, my son came home and sat down to devour the pork chops and a baked potato. He told me about his day.

Sabbath is a day when this working mom slows down enough to listen. To listen to a pear tree rattling in the wind. To listen to a daughter who is discovering who she is, and trying to figure out how to communicate that discovery on her college applications. To listen to a son who finds joy in spending most of his Sunday at church or in community. To listen to the voice of my own gladness, which calls me to the woods and to the backyard and to rest.

Sabbath for us is a sundown-to-sundown day, so technically, as soon as I need the lights on in the house, the day is over. Which is why I am back on the computer, writing this. And why the washing machine labors. And yet, the peace that the day of rest brought lingers like the fragrance of the wood-burning fireplace, companionable and warm.

This is just one snapshot from a family album of Sabbaths. I wrote it about five years ago. There are so many others. Some are not so idyllic, like those awkward family photos that everyone has—and the misguided share online? Those are in that Sabbath album, too; they might be filed under the heading "Sabbath fail." But Sabbath is a grace-soaked practice that you can't fail at. It's something you do over and over, never perfect, but always receive as a gift. It's an invitation to a journey, to try a different path or experiment with a new way. It's a sacred space in time.

Sabbath is more than a day. It is a way of life, a conviction we order our lives around, based on what we believe about God. But mostly, it is a gift from God we can't find time to open, because we don't know what we're missing.

## Practice, Not Perfect

I have been practicing Sabbath with my family for two decades, quite imperfectly, but always enthusiastically. We've learned a lot. I could not always get everyone on board. My husband is a Realtor, and often worked on Sundays. My kids played sports, so we sometimes spent an hour or two of our Sabbath sitting in bleachers at a volleyball tournament or soccer game. While our practice was never perfect, over time, we got it right more often than not, and leaned into grace when we didn't. That impacted my children in a good way.

When we first started experimenting with Sabbath, my children were babies, and I was a mom desperate for a break. Marriage was hard, full of arguments about who works harder, and both of us felt unappreciated. Sabbath offered a respite.

We mistakenly think we can't "do Sabbath" (another oxymoron) with small children. But toddlers are easy compared to Facebook, YouTube, and the countless other digital distractions. It's not our children who keep us from resting. It's the countless other distractions. Not only are we moving too fast, we are spinning our wheels. We need to find a way to slow both the MPHs and the RPMs of our lives.

Sabbath is not something we ever get perfect, any more than we get other practices perfect. My prayers are often ragged and messy, not perfect. My Bible-reading practice sometimes just confuses me—or gets woefully neglected. My solitude times can make me restless and fidgety. But I still engage in these practices, imperfectly, because the goal is not to get good at spiritual practices. The goal is to create some space for God in my life. Nothing has done that in quite the profound way that my imperfect, messy Sabbath keeping has.

## The Greatest Commandment

The truth driving our Sabbath rest (an oxymoron? how can rest be driven?) is the sufficiency of God's provision. We respond to the Almighty's generous provision with trust and our own willingness to be generous—extravagantly so—to ourselves and to the people around us. These two things, trust of God and generosity to neighbor, lie at the heart of the Sabbath. If you want to experience more of God and develop a genuine love for your neighbor, Sabbath may be the path to do so.

Sabbath invites us not just to take a day of rest but to embrace a theology of trust in God's provision, a theology that posits we have enough resources that we can afford to stop accumulating and striving for a day. We serve a God who does not demand that we work 24/7, but rather a God who rests and invites us to join in that rest with joy and gladness, and to extend that invitation to all—across all social boundaries of age, class, gender, income, race. Every week that we choose to rest for one day, we participate in a miracle: God takes our labor of six days, and multiplies it into provision for seven days.

To practice Sabbath is to obey what Jesus said was the greatest commandment: to love God and love your neighbor. The two are inseparable, like two sides of a coin. You cannot decide to love God and hate your neighbor, or even just ignore your neighbor. What does taking a day of rest have to do with loving your neighbor?

While I could write an entire book on Sabbath practice (and have, actually), I want to explain how Sabbath keeping reflects love of our neighbor by focusing on theology and practice. Theology is what we think and talk about; practice is what we do—our spirituality embodied. Theology and practice are inextricably linked. If we say we believe something but don't live it out, we don't actually believe it.

## A Sabbath Theology

Theology is what we talk about when we talk about God. Theology informs decisions we make, the way we live, the way we interact with other people and the world around us. Is God kind and gracious? Demanding and punitive? Impossible to please? Distant and aloof? Your answers to these kinds of questions make up your theology: how you see God, your perception of God's character. Your understanding of God is influenced by your faith tradition, teaching you've heard, books you've read, your relationships, especially with your parents.

A theology of Sabbath asks, What does Sabbath say about God? What does God tell us about Sabbath? What does Sabbath teach us about God? What truth about God does Sabbath keeping reveal?

In the Old Testament, we read that God tells the people of Israel to remember and observe the Sabbath. The Sabbath is not a capricious command, but one given to God's people so that they could understand God and themselves better, and so that they could flourish. It invites everyone to the table, to enjoy bread, wine, and fellowship, and in this way it foreshadows both later Jewish festivals and the Christian Eucharist. It invites everyone to rest. Sabbath is a practice that thumbs its nose at our hurried, frantic culture, offering us a respite in the midst of the chaos.

When we keep Sabbath, we make a theological statement to ourselves and others: God is trustworthy. I can trust in God's provision. I can stop and rest, and still know that God will love me and provide for me. I do not need to be afraid if I don't work on this day, because God can be trusted.

Sabbath is a day of rest, yet it's so much more than a day. It is the Fourth Command that hinges the Ten Commandments together. The first three are about our relationship with God (have no other gods, don't make idols, don't take God's name in vain). The last six are about our relationship with our neighbors (honor your parents, don't murder, don't commit adultery, don't steal, don't give false testimony, don't covet). Sabbath bridges these two subsets because it is about both relationships.

Walter Brueggemann, in his excellent short book *Sabbath as Resistance*, points out that the first three commandments not only instruct Israel in how to relate to God, but also provide a stark contrast to the gods and theology of Egypt, where Israel had been enslaved for centuries.

The first three commands reject the gods and pharaoh and the economics of Egypt, and introduce God, Yahweh, whose approval could not be earned—only received, as a gift, as a grace. God, curiously, also rests.

These commands are not just about how Israel is to behave. They define the nature of God and remind us that God is "embedded in narrative," Brueggemann writes.

The biblical text begins with, "I am the LORD your God, who brought you out of Egypt, out of the land of slavery. You shall have no other gods before me" (Exod. 20:2–3).

So before God tells the people what to do, God reminds them of what has already been done: they've been set free, brought out of Egypt. The commands begin with a reminder of our freedom.

Brueggemann notes that the economic structure of Egypt is one that never rested. It demanded more bricks from the Israelite slaves, more food for the pharaoh to hoard or to sacrifice to Egyptian gods. It was an economy with no days off, no rest. The economy was fueled by unwritten scarcity and stratified society. Despite the seeming abundance, the culture said there was never enough, and rest was not an option.

Does this sound familiar? We may have enough food and shelter and provision, yet we always want more. We live in a culture fueled by fear—fear that someone is going to take away what we have. We feel an acute scarcity of time—we never have enough of that, right? The Sabbath is countercultural for precisely these reasons, and it is so essential to the healing of our souls.

The commandments begin with the exodus narrative, with God referencing his actions to bring his people out of Egypt. He tells them their own story and reminds them of the favor they've received so far. We don't need other gods, because Yahweh can be trusted. The Sabbath commandment begins with the word *remember*. Don't forget your story, don't forget that you're a part of God's story: a God who both redeems and rests.

The truth of the first three commands set up the fourth, Brueggemann explains. "Thus the Sabbath commandment is drawn into the exodus narrative, for the God who rests is the God who emancipates *from slavery* and consequently *from the work system of Egypt* and *from the gods of Egypt* who require and legitimate that work system. . . . The reference to 'Egypt' indicates that the God of Sinai who gives the Ten Commandments is never simply a 'religious figure' but is always preoccupied with and attentive to socioeconomic practice and policy."[1]

Socioeconomics? Yes. If we think of Sabbath only as a day off, a day where we can take a break, we only see if from the surface. We miss out on understanding the theology and the transformative potential of this spiritual practice on the people around us. Again, theology is what we think about God, but it must inform how we live as a result. How we live includes our interactions with others, especially the poor.

"The work stoppage permits a waning of anxiety, so energy is redeployed to the neighborhood," Brueggemann writes. "The odd insistence of the God of Sinai is to counter *anxious productivity* with *committed neighborliness*. The latter practice does not produce so much; but it creates an environment of security and respect and dignity that redefines the human project."[2]

Sabbath asks us to answer the questions, who is God, and who is my neighbor? How am I to respond to each? What does "committed neighborliness" involve? How do we redeploy our energy to the neighborhood?

For me, it often means stopping to talk to my neighbors as I putter in the yard. It means walking over to my next door neighbor's house to sit on the front porch with a plate of snacks and a glass of wine to watch the sunset and enjoy a leisurely conversation. It also means arranging the rest of my week in ways that offer love to neighbors I might not easily notice: the poor, the hungry, the marginalized, the refugee.

If we see Sabbath keeping only as a day of restrictions, a list of things we can't do, we overlook the joy, the amazing opportunity for transformation. We miss out on the freedom that this command brings us. In this gift, love of God and love of neighbor converge in one beautiful practice. We do very little, but experience so much.

Sabbath allows us to notice our neighbors, our family, even strangers. It often involves a meal in which we gather family or friends around our table, look into their faces and hear their stories.

When we step toward a Sabbath practice, we take a step back from working, shopping, buying, rushing. Not because work or commerce are bad. They're not. In fact, Sabbath instructions in the Bible remind us that for six days, we are to work. Work is part of the Sabbath command. We're not to rest for seven days a week, or even three. We're to work for six, and rest for one. Just for that one day, we stop. We trust God's provision. We choose not to shop, because our shopping keeps our neighbor—that is, the minimum wage store clerk—from resting. We choose to believe that what we have right now is enough to get us through the next twenty-four hours, instead of buying into the lie that we need to work to earn enough to make it to Monday. Our buying and selling fuels our anxiety, and in choosing Sabbath, we choose to overcome that anxiety with shalom—peace. And we believe that trusting God this one day will help us trust every day.

Our work, as well as our constant need to check our e-mail, get a few things done, or run a few errands, fuels our fear of scarcity—that we don't have enough time, or resources, to provide for ourselves. Our fear keeps us from realizing that God is our provider. Our work and busyness squeezes God right out of the equation. It keeps us from resting in Shabbat Shalom—deep, restful peace where trust in God pervades our hearts—which is more than just rest or absence of conflict.

My Jewish friends welcome the Sabbath on Friday evenings with the Shema, the ancient prayer named for its first word in Hebrew, *Sh'ma*, which means "hear." In Hebrew, it is *Sh'ma Yisra'eil Adonai Eloheinu Adonai echad*, which means "Hear O Israel, the Lord our God, the Lord is One."

A friend would sing that Shabbat prayer over her children before bed on Friday evenings. She loved the soothing sounds that make up the word *Shema*: *Shhh. Mmmm. Ahhh.* The words of the prayer are a call to intentionality: "hear" is more profound than "listen." Jesus would often say, "He who has ears to hear, let him hear." It is a call to pay attention, to the meaning and gift of Sabbath.

Sabbath invites us to hear. To slow down and quiet down enough to hear God, but also to hear the cry of our neighbors who need, more than anything, to have love expressed in the form of attention to their physical needs, or to their story.

## Who Is My Neighbor?

The Sabbath command is the longest, because it answers the question asked of Jesus centuries later—who is my neighbor?

It also forces us to consider, in practical terms, who is my God? Is God trustworthy? Will God provide? Do I believe this? If so, I should be able to set aside acquiring and striving and worrying for a day. If I do so for one day, perhaps my other days will be changed.

Here is the text, from Exodus, of the Sabbath command:

"Remember the Sabbath day by keeping it holy. Six days you shall labor and do all your work, but the seventh day is a sabbath to the LORD your God. On it you shall not do any work, neither you, nor your son or daughter, nor your male or female servant, nor your animals, nor any foreigner residing in your towns. For in six days the LORD made the heavens and the earth, the sea, and all that is in them, but he rested on the seventh day. Therefore the LORD blessed the Sabbath day and made it holy" (Exod. 20:8–11).

The Sabbath is not just a day off for privileged people, it is a reminder that rest is for everyone. All will rest—rich or poor, male or female, Jew or Gentile (foreigner), slave or free, human or animal, even. It foreshadows the oneness and egalitarianism that Christ brings: "There is neither Jew nor Gentile, neither slave nor free, nor is there male and female, for you are all one in Christ Jesus" (Gal. 3:28).

In the Deuteronomy version of the Ten Commandments, Sabbath is also the longest and most inclusive (even more so than Exodus, as it mentions specific animals who are also to be given a day off!). But rather than looking back to creation, commanding us to rest because God rested, it says, "Remember that you were slaves in Egypt and that the LORD your God brought you out of there with a mighty hand and an outstretched arm. Therefore the LORD your God has commanded you to observe the Sabbath day" (Deut. 5:15).

Observe the Sabbath because you were slaves? Of course. Slaves cannot take a day off. So if you can't take a day off, then perhaps you should ask, whose slave am I? What enslaves me? (Maybe my work, my phone, other people's opinions.) How can I be set free from this slavery? And how can I offer rest to those who are now in slavery, or who serve me?

Sabbath is faith embedded in practice. We cannot claim to believe in Sabbath but then neglect the practice of it. That's like saying "I believe exercise is important" while you sit on the couch. We have to go beyond liking the idea of a day of rest. We must actually rest—even if doing so stirs anxiety or fear. Fortunately, because of grace, we have a lot of leeway to figure out how to keep it, what our Sabbath practice will look like. We can let God customize our Sabbath—guiding us by the Holy Spirit into a life-giving practice that refrains from what is holding us in bondage. Engaging in this practice will renew us and bring us life. Sabbath is not just a day, but a command. To keep the Sabbath is to take and hold the gift that God has given. As in, *No really, you can keep it. It's yours, a gift of time. You thought you didn't have time, but now you do, a gift of a day. Keep it. Really.*

## An Invitation to Intimacy

On the seventh day of creation, the Bible says repeatedly, God rested. He created people on the sixth day, and then, declaring it very good, he rested. Long before the Ten Commandments or any other laws, God instituted Sabbath.

Rest is not the same thing as solitude, for God or for human beings. God rested in community with the world and creatures. Think of it: human beings, newly hewn from the dust, walking through the garden, conversing with God as they saw the amazing beauty of the world for the first time. Theologian Karl Barth says that on that first Sabbath, "love took form as time shared."

In keeping Sabbath, we get a glimpse of that intimacy. We can hang out with God, knowing we're loved without needing to perform, accomplish, or accumulate. Rest might include a good night's sleep, or even an afternoon nap. But it also includes time together, time in relationship with people we love. This is the kind of rest God enjoyed on Sabbath.

God rested. What an odd thing for God to do, really. The Egyptian gods did not rest, Brueggemann notes. Those gods, always pushing, demanding, striving, never stopped, never rested. But Yahweh was, and is, different. Our culture, like that ancient one, is always throbbing, pushing, demanding. We can shop and work and strive 24/7, and we often feel like we must do so. Into that culture, so similar to our own, comes a God who rests:

"God rested on the seventh day," Brueggemann writes. "God did not show up to do more. God absented God's self from the office. God did not come and check on creation in anxiety to be sure it was all working. God has complete confidence in the fruit-bearing, blessing-generating processes of creation that have been instituted. God exhibits no anxiety about the life-giving capacity of creation."[3]

God invites Israel, and us, to a similar attitude of trust. To absent ourselves from the office, to relax and quit checking on everything, as if our checking could do anything anyway. God invites his people to let go of anxiety and worry. Centuries later, God's message hadn't changed: "Come to me, all you who are weary and burdened, and I will give you rest" (Matt. 11:28).

We long to experience God's unconditional love. But if we never stop running and performing and achieving and working—how can we actually experience pure grace? How can we know God loves us when we don't do those things? Until we stop doing them, we have not truly tested God's love to see if indeed it keeps coming, even when we stop. Sabbath is truly a day to "taste and see that the LORD is good" (Ps. 34:8).

## The Freedom We Fear

I recently stood in front of a group of adults who had just heard a message on Sabbath, asking them to debrief and discuss. I'd asked two questions: What appealed to them about Sabbath? What barriers did they see to practicing it?

Almost everyone skipped the first question and went directly into their objections: Why this practice was just too hard, or their life was simply too busy to take a whole day to rest. Why it was an Old Testament thing, no longer required or even relevant, kind of like sacrificing goats or something. They'd listed reasons why they couldn't, even if they wanted to. They ignored my question about their desire, their longing for rest.

We all do this. We keep rushing and stay distracted, in part to avoid thinking about the desires of our heart. We don't want to admit that we sometimes, late at night, think, There's got to be more than this. We want more of God, a more meaningful life. But we don't want to ask for it. We get a little nervous about what would be involved, so we miss out on what God wants to give us.

What's true of the Christian life in general is especially true of Sabbath: it's not that it's been tried and found lacking; it's that it's never really been tried.[4]

Most of the folks in that room expressed curiosity about Sabbath but didn't know how to approach it. We're talking about people at church on a Sunday—they'd engaged in that much Sabbath, showing up and even carving out some extra time for a postservice discussion. But the prospect of an entire day of rest was daunting to them. They wanted to know how to do Sabbath, but they seemed sure they could not.

Some had baggage from a legalistic childhood that made them think Sabbath was simply a day of restriction that did not allow for any fun.

Sabbath is a hard practice, not because of its restrictions but because it has so much freedom. Sabbath has often been associated with legalism and rules that feel like the opposite of freedom. We are often both hungry for rules, yet resistant to them.

I believe it is not Sabbath rules but the lack of rules that keep us from even trying this life-giving practice. We're just not sure what to do with all that freedom. It leaves too many things open. When there's not one right way to do something, our questions about it can trip us up. We read about the Sabbath practice of other traditions, such as Judaism or Seventh-Day Adventist, and we think our Sabbath must conform to those standards, even though those two traditions are different. Within Judaism there are many different levels of orthodoxy and practice.

Can we garden? Is it okay to shop? Can my kids play soccer or do homework? What is allowed? We crave rules, but before we even get them, we object to them, calling them a barrier to our spiritual practice. We give up on Sabbath before we even begin.

This struggle to clarify and heed rules is nothing new. Even Jesus wrestled with it. Jesus drew a wide variety of critiques from religious leaders, but they were especially persnickety about the way he observed Sabbath. Reading through the gospels, it almost seems that Jesus is on a mission to redefine Sabbath, to break the rules and rewrite them. Why was Sabbath what got Jesus in trouble the most?

Sabbath was a boundary marker for the Jews of Jesus's time. Jesus was Jewish. It was easy to critique him on Sabbath keeping because of the many rules associated with it, which of course raised the odds of rule breaking.

Every law in the Old Testament serves as an archetype, a prophetic symbol, of the coming Messiah. The sacrifice of a perfect lamb, the blood on the doorposts at Passover, the first fruits of the harvest: all carry a messianic meaning. Sabbath, a day in which we cease striving and rest in God, offers a prophetic picture of grace. We rest, not because we've earned it, or even because we're exhausted, but because of God's unmerited favor. Jesus embodied that Sabbath grace and reminded people of God's original intent.

Jesus was the *fulfillment* of the Sabbath command. He said it himself, "Come to me, and I will give you rest." He was Sabbath personified, embodied. He was remaking Sabbath, how it was practiced, and what it ultimately meant. Sabbath is a day to lean into grace.

Jesus had a lot to say about Sabbath, things like "The Sabbath was made for man [meaning human beings], not man for the Sabbath" (Mark 2:27). In other words, the Sabbath was made for, and given to, people. It's a gift. We don't need to be a slave to Sabbath, but rather, we can enjoy it.

We live in that grace, now, rather than under the law. The Sabbath commandment is one we technically can ignore because it's not something upon which our salvation depends. But we do so at our own peril. When we reject this gift, we miss not just an opportunity to de-stress or relax, but an opportunity to experience the *rest* of God, the part we've missed. Author Mark Buchanan turns this into a play on words, as he writes, "The rest of God—the rest God gladly gives so that we might discover that part of God we're missing—is not a reward for finishing. It's not a bonus for work well done. It's sheer gift. It is a stop-work order in the midst of work that's never complete, never polished. Sabbath is not the break we're allotted at the tail end of completing all our tasks and chores, the fulfillment of all our obligations. It's the rest we take smack-dab in the middle of them, without apology, without guilt, and for no better reason than God told us we could."⁵

## Limits, Chores, and Delegation

The Hebrew word *Shabbat* simply means "to cease, to stop." When we Sabbath, we just stop. Not because we're done, but because God invites us to take a break, to set aside our work, our fear, our anxiety. We are invited to rest both our bodies and our minds, to leave what is undone until tomorrow.

That's hard for us. We're hurried; we're used to rushing and working and striving. But we didn't get this stressed or hurried overnight. It's not like we were calm, rested people and then woke up one day hurried and bothered. Our hurry sickness crept up on us gradually. And we may have to reverse those habits gradually. Sabbath requires us to trust.

If the rest of our life is overscheduled, Sabbath may seem impossible. If we are doing too much, it will be hard to create God space one day per week.

Whether you are single or married, have young children or an empty nest, don't say yes to things that will prevent you from taking a day off. Don't sign up for too many activities, or take on an extra project at work, or cram your week with too many obligations.

Two very practical changes helped us build a Sabbath habit as a family. They had nothing to do with Sundays, but with redistributing the family workload. Managing and running a home is a full-time job. Caring for small children is another full-time job. Working moms juggle three full-time jobs unless they can delegate some of that work to other family members, or to hired help, or if other family members volunteer to help out. Don't hold your breath for the latter to happen, especially if those family members are teenagers.

So once my kids could reach the buttons on the washer and dryer, they had to do their own laundry and clean their own rooms, and help with the general housekeeping. We also developed a chore chart so that each of my children, and my husband, had to do a chore for the week: dishes, vacuuming, bathroom cleaning, whatever. Both my kids were in sports, which meant they were now responsible for washing their sweaty, icky uniforms in time for their next game. This alone gave my soul joy.

Delegating is a spiritual practice. If one person in your family is doing everyone else's laundry and all the other housework, plus holding down a job outside the home, finding the margin for Sabbath becomes incredibly challenging. Delegate laundry. Share the housework. Train up your children. When your kids go to college or move out on their own, they'll thank you. And when you only have to do your own laundry and not your teenager's, you will be dancing around the laundry room.

Second, we protected the overall pace of our lives by saying no to overscheduling. Don't be afraid to place loving limits on activities: yours and your kids'. Don't buy into the lie that more activity means more opportunity, and that your child will somehow miss out if they don't do everything.

Our kids were allowed to do one sport at a time, and one artistic pursuit, such as art class or piano lessons. That limit impacts the number of times you're running to practices and so on during the week, and it's less likely that you'll be driving from a soccer game to a volleyball practice to a band recital, all in one day. If you have a large family, one sport per child can still multiply into a busy life, but at least it provides limits. If you slow down your week, your Sabbath will be easier to implement.

In other words, love and setting limits with your family will move you toward Sabbath Simplicity. It will create God space in your life—and your laundry room.

Start slowly, and build a practice over time. Give yourself several weeks or even months to experiment and play with a Sabbath practice. Start small, with one thing you'll do and one thing you won't do. That is, one thing to engage in on Sabbath and one thing to refrain from.

## What Should You Engage In?

Rest doesn't mean sitting and staring at the walls. Engage in activities that bring joy or refreshment. Begin by asking yourself, what is one thing I wish I had more time for? Maybe it's talking with a friend, or going for a walk or a run. Maybe it's time to hang out with your family somewhere other than the minivan. Maybe you wish you had time for family meals or to read your Bible or some other inspiring book. So do one of those things—and resist the urge to try to do all of those things, all at once!

Maybe instead of watching the nature channel, you'll actually go outside and experience nature firsthand. Even if you live in the city, you can see squirrels in the park, or bugs on the sidewalk.

Maybe you'll introduce yourself to a neighbor you don't know. Maybe you'll take a nap, or read a book that challenges you to think. You are free to do that, or not.

Maybe you've read all the research on family meals and wish you could fit that into your life. What if you did a family meal on Sabbath? It doesn't have to be homemade, it just needs to be shared with your family, around a table instead of in front of the television or in the car.

In the Jewish tradition, the Sabbath is welcomed by the woman of the home—the wife, mom, or grandmother. She lights candles and says a prayer. Then her husband blesses her, and their children. Why not try lighting candles, and speaking a blessing to the people around your table? Not sure how to bless? Just say, "I'm thankful for you. One thing I really love about you is…" and fill in the blanks with affirming words about that person, their faith, their character. Many Jewish families use Proverbs 31 as a script for the husband to read, affirming his wife.

Again, we have freedom. You don't have to do these things, but which of them appeals to you most? Where did you think, I want that?

Start there. With your desire. With your longing for something meaningful. What one thing would make your life more satisfying, more meaningful? That desire was given to you by God. God longs to fulfill it. God invites you to move gently toward that desire.

On Sabbath, do that one thing that would bring you joy, that would feel restful and meaningful, or just fun, even if you think you don't have time for it. Just for an hour, set aside time to do something life-giving. Open the gift of time and use it for what your heart longs for.

If you're married, maybe you're so busy you think that you don't have time for sexual intimacy. The ancient rabbis recommended that married couples enjoy lovemaking—truly a gift from God—as part of their Sabbath practice. Maybe that's another reason Sabbath traditionally begins at sundown?

## What Do You Wish You Could Be Free Of?

Maybe it's housework, or e-mail, or worry. Choose, for one day, to refrain from that chore, that obligation. Let it go, trust that the work, the busyness, the e-mail, and the dirty laundry will still be there tomorrow. Let God hold it for you while you rest, and while you engage in what gives you joy.

Many people, even if they are not part of any faith tradition, take what is called a "digital Sabbath." Interestingly, the people leading this charge work in the tech industry. A digital Sabbath is simply taking a break from technology. You unplug, turn off phones, tablets, computers, for an entire day. Even if they aren't turning off their cell phones for God, these pioneers have tapped into the reality of how we were created. Human beings, made in the image of a God who rests, function best when they take a day off once a week to rest. Trading screen time for face time heals our souls.

## Cease. Embrace. Sundown to Sundown.

Over the next several weeks, continue to engage in your thing you love, and cease from doing the thing you want freedom from. Slowly add to your practice. One more thing to be free of, one more thing to engage in. Edit if necessary: if you try something and it doesn't fit, let it go.

As Mark Buchanan writes, "So I submit this as Sabbath's golden rule: *Cease from what is necessary. Embrace that which gives life. And then do whatever you want.*"[6]

In most Sabbath traditions, the day does not begin at sunrise or even midnight, but at sunset. By Jewish tradition, it ends the next day once three stars are visible in the evening sky, so a bit after sunset. I highly recommend following this ancient practice. Slowing down just as dusk approaches feels more natural for most of us. Trust me, a sundown-to-sundown time frame makes it easier to begin building a Sabbath habit. How hard is it to engage in a practice that begins with a meal followed by sleep?

Consider the following time framework for Sabbath, and build on it in whatever way fits your life and your faith. You do not have to use this framework. It is one possibility you can consider using or adapting according to God's leading, your own personality, and your season of life.

## Framework to Build On

Traditionally, the day before Sabbath is Preparation Day. So prepare. Prior to sunset, spend some time tidying your house and preparing a meal to share with your family. If cooking is not your jam, grab a premade meal at Costco and have it ready so you don't need to shop on Sunday. In our home, Saturday afternoon is devoted to cleaning and de-cluttering so that we can enjoy Sabbath in a restful space.

If you have them, involve your kids in this preparation. Promise that they'll have time with you, and your attention without distraction, if they will help you clean and prepare.

Consider making something that can be enjoyed as leftovers the next day so that whoever does the cooking in your house can have a break from that job. If you're superorganized, cook something on Friday that can be popped into the oven on Sunday. If you're not, two words: Stouffer's Lasagna.

Turn off your computer before sunset, and remind yourself to leave it off until tomorrow evening. You may even want to pray, just briefly, thanking God for the computer, and asking God for help in letting the computer rest for a day.

As evening begins, light candles and enjoy a meal with friends or family. Around the table, talk about ideas or questions of faith. Read a short passage of Scripture. Speak a blessing on your spouse and children. Love the people around your table by listening to them.

Have everyone help clean up. Even small children can put their plates and utensils in the sink or dishwasher.

Spend the evening relaxing by reading, having a conversation, or even going to bed early. If you have small kids, play a game with them or read them a story. Give them the gift of your attention.

Many summer Saturday evenings find us on our next door neighbor's front porch, where we pour some wine and share some snacks and just hang out and talk. We have lived here for years, and the community we share on the porch is strong. It often feels like a deeper connection than what I find at church. Sometimes we laugh, sometimes we have some deep conversations. Usually both.

Wake up the next day, and you are already halfway through your Sabbath! That wasn't so hard, was it? And now, you have a day to spend with God and with others, resting.

Worship God in the morning, whether by attending church or studying the Bible on your own, or with a group.

Eat leftovers or make sandwiches, or let your family graze on snacks and simple food prepared ahead of time.

Take a walk, or go for a run or bike ride, if that's something you find enjoyable.

Take a nap.

Engage in something that brings you joy.

Read something inspirational. If you like to journal, do so. If you hate journaling, don't do it and don't worry about it. Write down one quote from what you read, and share it with your family at mealtime.

Don't do chores or laundry. Don't check Facebook or your e-mail. Keep the computer off. Pray for the strength to let these things go. Unplug, literally.

Instead of digital interaction or chores, have a face-to-face interaction with someone you love: play with your child without doing something else at the same time, or make love to your spouse, or have a cup of coffee or tea with your neighbor. If you live alone, invite a friend to hang out or go for a walk with you. Get outside, and look at the beauty of the trees or birds or even the faces of ordinary humans on the streets of your city, all made in the image of God.

Spend some time praying for your neighbors, and for those less fortunate than yourself.

As the sun sets, thank God for the gift of rest. Use the remaining hours of the evening to prepare for the week ahead.

# Hospitality

## *Space in My Home*

All over my house, people are sleeping. Nearly all of them were strangers until a few days ago. I'm sipping coffee as golden light filters through the tree line along the back fence. Through the open windows, birdsong blends with the far-off roar and clunking of the garbage truck making its Monday morning rounds through our suburban neighborhood.

I love the quiet of summer mornings, but I also love having a house full of guests. I'm enjoying both right now.

My dearest and closest college friend Sandy has a daughter, Lucy, who is twenty-one, right between my two kids in age. I've known Lucy since she was a baby, even though they live in another state. Lucy leads a band that played at Chicago's Lollapalooza music festival on its opening day. What an amazing opportunity! Lucy's career is just beginning and funds are tight, so she and the band search for cheap accommodations while on tour. Since family and friends are always at the top of the list, she and her band members stayed with us. They arrived Thursday, then went back to Chicago for a few days.

Last night, all six of them came to get a night's sleep before they hit the road to drive across the country for their next gig.

I cut up some fruit and set out some zucchini bread so they can help themselves to some breakfast. They wake up one by one, wandering downstairs bed-headed and bleary-eyed. Most accept mugs of coffee that I offer. A few are literally eating cantaloupe out of the bowl with their fingers, ignoring the spoons and smaller serving bowls I've set on the counter. They're talking and drinking coffee and packing; it's chaos of a lovely sort. I'm learning their names and what each of them does—drummer, bass guitarist, manager.

Some of us wish we could get closer to Jesus, but when he invites us to do so by welcoming strangers, we beg off. *That's not my gift*, or *I'm an introvert*, we say. When we decline this invitation, Jesus does not love us any less. He never withholds grace. But we miss an opportunity to experience divine presence, perhaps wrapped in a bed-headed indie rock band.

Hospitality is openness, being willing to say, "Sure—come on in." There is room at the table, or on my couch, for you. It's letting twentysomethings eat cantaloupe like popcorn. Martha Stewart might be horrified. Which is exactly how I know it's the right thing to do. Small but meaningful touches gather people in and tell them you've thought about their comfort, that you're glad they are there. Not perfection, but little things: a pile of fluffy white towels in the bathroom, or zucchini bread pulled from the oven an hour or two before they arrive so that the house itself extends a cinnamon-y welcome. At its best, hospitality makes people feel as if they've come home, as if they can put their feet up on the coffee table. (I purposely have foot-friendly coffee tables—you can find them at thrift stores everywhere.) Hospitality is not about perfection or impressing; it invites people into a space where they can be themselves, unedited, comfy, welcomed.

## Jesus Both Offered and Received Hospitality

For much of his ministry, Jesus was an itinerant rabbi. He described himself at one point as homeless—he depended on the hospitality of strangers and friends (such as Mary, Martha, and Lazarus). However, he did serve large meals once in a while, turning just a few loaves and fishes into a meal for thousands. He provided some extra wine for a wedding once. Religious leaders of his day accused Jesus of practicing the wrong kind of hospitality: "This man welcomes sinners and eats with them," they muttered, because tax collectors and sinners gathered to hear Jesus.

The word that translates to "welcomes" (*prosdechomai*) is not a passive word, but an active one, connoting private access, acceptance, and companionship. To welcome sinners and eat with them went beyond hospitality to alignment and full acceptance. Jesus embodied his spirituality, gathering at table and breaking bread. He didn't just talk about love, he actually loved. We have the opportunity every day to welcome sinners as Jesus did, and in fact to welcome them as if they were Jesus.

We can ask the well-worn question, "What would Jesus do?" The relevant question when it comes to hospitality is this: "What if this were Jesus?" What if this person at my door, this family member at my table, this stranger looking for shelter, the refugee coming to a new city, were Jesus? How can we welcome others as if they were Jesus? After all, he does say what we do for others we've done for him.

## Welcoming Strangers

This afternoon I will do several loads of laundry, washing the sheets and towels, remaking the beds, preparing for the next round of guests, the first of whom will arrive in a few days. I will live my faith by making beds and hanging towels on the rack. Summer seems to be the time when people end up on my couch, our guest room, or, now that my kids are off on their own, in our extra bedrooms. A year ago we had my daughter and a slew of her college friends here in May, followed a steady rotation of guests throughout the summer. But this week, my daughter signed a lease for an apartment in Los Angeles. Her friends are less likely to be here—but they know they are welcome. Her college roommate stayed for a night on her cross-country drive to grad school in New Jersey just a few weeks ago.

The transition to empty nest was not easy. It was helpful to use my friend Tim's descriptor: the spacious nest. My husband Scot and I are still in it, after all. It's not empty completely.

As I readied last week for Lucy's arrival, moving my desk against the wall so I could put the air mattress on the floor in my office, I thought that maybe in launching my kids, I gained two guest rooms. I still miss my kids terribly, although we talk and text often. But I'm here in Chicago, and they're both on the west coast. My husband and I have a five-bedroom house. We use two of those bedrooms, one for sleeping and one for my office. Most of the time, the extra space echoes. But I sense that God is asking us to take the next step in opening our home to people who need respite on a deeper level.

We moved to this house from a slightly smaller one a few blocks away, where we had lived for about eight years. We live within an hour's drive of where each of us grew up. Yes, we're settled here. Some people move frequently, have lived in cities all around the country, or even all over the world. We are not those kind of people. Self-employed, we have never been transferred. I have a few dozen friends here that I've known for more than two decades. I rarely have to use a map or GPS when I drive, because I know Chicago and its suburbs like I know the way around my own house.

But from that settled, deep-rooted place, we are people who open our doors. We engage in what Henri Nouwen and others called a ministry of presence: one in which we strive to know and love our neighbors, open our doors to strangers, pray for our city, and simply be with people.

We moved to our current home seventeen years ago because I needed an office, since I work from home. We also wanted to respond to what I can only call an "invitation to invite."

Jesus once told his followers: "To those who use well what they are given, even more will be given, and they will have an abundance.... For I was hungry, and you fed me. I was thirsty, and you gave me a drink. I was a stranger, and you invited me into your home. I was naked, and you gave me clothing. I was sick, and you cared for me. I was in prison, and you visited me" (Matt. 25:29, 35–36 NLT).

When we bought this home, we had a strong sense that God wanted us to share it, to invite others in, to gather people together. What did it mean to welcome strangers into our home? Whether for an afternoon, an evening, or a bit longer, we have tried to figure out what it means to steward our home. It's something God provided and asked us to use well. Like the servants who are asked to invest the Master's treasure, we are trying to use our home to bring about kingdom returns.

That had already been a practice in our other home, where we had occasionally hosted people, sometimes for a month or two at a time, before we had children.

We'd always led small groups in our home, and continued to practice that type of hospitality—gathering people around the table to study and share our lives. But we felt called to open our home more. *Called* might seem a strange word when you're talking about your home, but calling is the only word that fits.

Jesus said, "I was a stranger and you invited me into your home." That "inviting" is not just about offering people a place to crash. The original language conveys a gathering in, joining together, welcoming. How exactly could we do that? How could our rootedness provide a safe place not only for people to stay, but to be gathered in and welcomed? In other words, what would a ministry of place look like in the suburbs of Chicago?

At the time, in 2002, our church hosted a number of conferences each year, where pastors from around the country and even around the world would gather for training, encouragement, worship. Each conference would draw thousands of people to our church campus from around the country and even around the world.

Our church offered international pastors the opportunity to stay in homes of church members for free. We signed up as soon as we heard about the opportunity to host, and our first guest, Svein-Tony, from Norway, arrived in February.

I explained to the kids that a person was coming stay with us, in the bedroom in the basement, and he was traveling a long way to come to visit. Norway, I said, was on the "other side of the world."

"The other side of the world?" my daughter asked, frowning at our apparent recklessness. "Does he *know* Osama bin Laden??" After the attack of September 11, 2001, we'd tried to reassure our kids that they were safe, because the people who'd flown the planes were not going to come to our town, that their leader was "on the other side of the world." (I admit, in hindsight, this was not the best way to explain the situation. But what can I say? We all had a bit of PTSD going on at that time. We did the best we could.) So now, just a few months after that attack, we were opening our home to strangers from other lands.

The kids were also at the age when they'd been learning about "stranger danger" in school. So now, their crazy parents were inviting a stranger—from the other side of the world, no less—to stay in our home?

We pulled out the globe and found Norway, pointing out that it was actually not in the Middle East, and using a teachable moment to explain that, yes, there are bad people in the world, but there are mostly good people, everywhere—even in the same town as bin Laden.

Aaron, who was only five at the time, listened intently, without comment. At school the day after Svein-Tony arrived, he told his kindergarten teacher, "Mrs. Spaletto, I've got a

Norwegian in my basement." She called me that afternoon to report this adorable conversation, and, I think, to make sure that we were not involved in international kidnapping or something.

Thus began a wonderful season of welcoming international guests, from all over "the other side of the world," including England, South Africa, Ireland, France, Germany, Brazil, Australia. Each year, we'd host for several conferences held at our church, including the Global Leadership Summit, a two-day leadership conference that draws more than 10,000 leaders to our church, and is simulcast to an estimated 160,000 people.

Then, our basement flooded, and the recession hit. We turned down requests to host because our basement was in disarray and needed to be fixed. We could not afford to remodel it. Because... recession. Because... both of us self-employed. Because... things got hard for a while, but not just financially. We lost our way with hospitality. We got out of practice while struggling to stay afloat and to stay married. Those were hard years. We slogged through a really hard season in our marriage, distracted ourselves with our children's activities, told ourselves we were too busy to extend hospitality.

Without a shared practice of hospitality to ground us, to connect us, Scot and I redirected our focus to the kids, our work, and other distractions—including our financial struggles. The basement, with half of its carpeting torn up and the paneling pulled off the walls, was that project that never got done, mocking us, causing stress, and provoking more than a few arguments. The shared joy of hospitality got sidetracked, and we suffered for it. Our financial struggles and lack of a shared practice of hospitality became a downward spiral. During that season, we said no to a lot of hospitality opportunities. I regret not understanding then that hospitality does not mean offering perfection.

Here was what I discovered: Jesus still welcomes me, even if I cannot muster the strength to welcome others. But if I embrace the inconvenience of welcoming others—even into my messy, under-construction life—I get to know the truth: Hospitality is not about me, not about entertaining, not about impressing anyone. It is to experience God's presence in a profound way.

Finally, things began to turn around—financially, relationally, spiritually. We got back on track in a number of ways. We got some help, relationally and spiritually. We healed up a bit. We got our basement renovation finished and found ourselves eager, once again, to open our home.

## Get Your House in Order

While you can't let imperfections be an excuse for bowing out of hospitality, sometimes you need to do some repairs. If the people you live with are not feeling safe and welcomed, even if it's partly their own fault, you may need to focus on them first. You may need to get your own house in order. The question is not do I offer hospitality, but rather, to *whom* do I offer hospitality?

Sometimes you need to offer hospitality to your own family, to create some space for healing and listening to one another's stories. That season was hard, but necessary. We had to realign ourselves with one another and with God before we were able to provide a welcoming space. Not a perfect space, but one that was safe and not wrapped in thick, unspoken tension. Okay, not always unspoken. Sometimes spoken, loudly. Who would want to come stay in the middle of that?

But if we wait until we get things perfectly together, we may never feel okay about braving hospitality. I wish we'd been brave enough to invite people to stay even when our basement was torn up and our marriage had a few tatters. Because now I know that hospitality can actually bring the healing we seek, to our homes and families. As Parker Palmer wrote,

> Hospitality means inviting the stranger into our private space, whether that be the space of our own home or the space of our personal awareness and concern. And when we do so, some important transformations occur. Our private space is suddenly enlarged; no longer tight and cramped and restricted, but open and expansive and free.[1]

Eventually, we began to say yes again to hosting, welcoming people from around the world even as our oldest was leaving the nest. And indeed, this "enlarged our space" in a way that surprised us all.

Last year, we hosted Nikola, a young pastor from Macedonia, while he attended the Global Leadership Summit at our church. Hearing the story of our hosting adventures, and Aaron's comment to his teacher all those years ago, he began to refer to himself as "the Macedonian in the basement."

Nikola recently e-mailed me and asked if he could stay with us again, when he attends the summit this year. I of course said yes. He will be here next weekend. The church also asked us if we'd host another guest, or maybe two, and since I now have extra guest rooms, I agreed.

It's hard to explain how I felt when I got the e-mail saying we'd not only have Nikola, but also Fabian from Quito, Ecuador, and Azar from Nazareth, Israel. *Giddy* would not be too strong a word. A quiet joy welled up in me, and I felt very grateful that we'd found our way back to the practice of hospitality.

Hospitality is easy for me, because it is not entertaining or trying to impress. Sure, I've got to wash the sheets and make up the beds. I'll probably bake a few things so that we can have some nice breakfast options. I like to cook; that's how I express love. But hospitality should never be confused with entertaining. This is not a Pinterest post, it's a spiritual practice—a way for us to create some space for God in our lives. As Jesus said, "I was a stranger and you welcomed me." When Scot and I see people in the guest room or around our table as *Jesus*, it changes everything.

Our thirty-year-old suburban tract house is modest. The rooms are small. The ceilings are not cathedral and they don't soar. The kitchen has never been remodeled, the furniture is mostly second-hand, except for a few key pieces that we bought at IKEA. The window treatments are all from Target. The television, which refuses to wear out, is twenty-five years old, and we don't have cable. The artwork on the walls is mostly photos taken by my daughter, paintings or sketches my son created, and family photos. It's homey, simple, a little cluttered. There are a lot of books, and occasional piles of paper, and a jumble of shoes under a side table in the front foyer.

That doesn't matter to us, or to pastors who are grateful for a place to stay. The back deck looks out at a little slice of woods, where birds and squirrels chatter. And the neighborhood is friendly—we know all our neighbors and actually spend time with them, which is another often-overlooked aspect of hospitality. We're about two miles from church, making our location perfect for guests who attend the summit.

The practice of hospitality provides a sense of place, makes ordinary time and space sacred. Rather than seeking to impress people, it aims to welcome Jesus, disguised as an ordinary person. It creates a space where guests can share their stories around a table, where they can laugh, and where they can find rest, be it in a well-worn chair by the fire, a lawn chair on our deck, or on an air mattress on the floor.

## Welcome to the Table

The summer before my daughter left for college, we did not host for the summit, but attended it. Our pastor reminded the congregation: We have a lot of people who are from all over the globe attending. Welcome them. The international guests wear name tags that show what country they're from. Notice those name tags, go out of your way to say hello, to offer assistance if they need it.

Our daughter Melanie, her friend Jonathan, and Jonathan's parents, Jane and John, all attended with us. We'd planned to have them over for dinner after the day's sessions, so I had beef stew in the Crock-Pot.

Somehow during our conversations, Melanie and I came up with the idea of not just saying hello to internationals, but inviting some to dinner at our house that evening. We missed having guests. It might have been a bit inconvenient to add two guests to the table, but I wanted my kids to welcome strangers, and the adventure of inviting some just sounded too fun to pass up.

During a break, we looked for people with international name tags, and tried to get into conversations (without seeming too creepy), but nothing was clicking. The afternoon session started, and we went to our seats, but I didn't see my husband Scot. Five minutes after the session began, he slipped into the seat beside me. "I found some Canadians," he whispered loudly. "They're coming to dinner!"

I texted my son, who'd been at work, but was now at home. "We're bringing some people home for dinner, can you set the table for nine? And maybe clean up a little bit?" When your sixteen-year-old can handle this assignment without questioning, you know hospitality is your family's thing, not just your own.

Two Canadian pastors, who later admitted our invitation alarmed them slightly, overcame their trepidation and came to dinner. I added a bit more broth to the stew, pulled out an extra loaf of bread, and prayed a loaves-and-fishes type of blessing on it. Everyone had enough to eat, but the conversation was what satisfied us all the most. We heard about these kind pastors' work at their churches in Canada, so we talked about insights gained from the teaching in the conference.

At one point Jane, Jonathan's mom, said, "Mel and Jonathan, you're leaving for college in a few weeks. What will you miss the most?" Mel looked around the table, lifted her hands and swept them in circles, motioning to all of us around the table, and said, "This." This table, this place where we gather strangers and friends until we can't tell which is which. This table, where we always welcomed her friends, her brother's friends, neighbors, visitors from a dozen countries. This table, where we quietly remind ourselves that it is Jesus we serve and listen to. This meal, extended to feed two more with a little more water and salt and bread. This.

Welcoming strangers from around the world has not always been easy or convenient. But my daughter was marked by our doing so. She began to see that people from "the other side of the world" are friendly, are not so different from us, and tell interesting stories. She began to appreciate the things we have in common, and the things we don't. Before she graduated from high school, she'd been to South Africa and Spain. She's twenty-two now and has traveled to a dozen countries in Europe, as well as two in Africa. She's planning to travel to Peru next month. She speaks Spanish and is comfortable in a variety of cultures, from the backcountry of Yosemite National Park to the west side of Chicago to South Central Los Angeles.

I texted her while writing this chapter to ask what impact hosting internationals had on her. Her response: "I think more than anything, hosting international guests made me more interested in people from different parts of the world. It fueled curiosity. I learned at a young age that not everyone lives the same way—something likely rare for kids who grew up in my fairly homogeneous suburb—and I became more interested in how others lived."

Obviously, being part of a large church that hosts an international conference and screens our guests is part of why it's easy for us to engage in that particular iteration of hospitality.

However, there are other avenues to explore if you don't have that option. Every meal is a chance to practice hospitality.

## Family Meals

Sometimes, hospitality begins with your own family, your own community. The early church, described in Acts, gathered around tables, not just to have a cube of white bread and a thimbleful of grape juice. They gathered for meals as a community, as a family. The Bible describes them in this way: "Every day they continued to meet together in the temple courts. They broke bread in their homes and ate together with glad and sincere hearts, praising God and enjoying the favor of all the people" (Acts 2:46–47). Meals, even with the people closest to us, are a practice of hospitality that we can embrace, with friends or family.

Our regular meals can be a hurried routine, or they can be a chance to experience intimacy with God. How will we frame these moments around the table? Will we see them for what they are: chances to form our hearts and the hearts of our friends, children, and extended family?

The research on family meals is clear: kids do better if they gather around a table with their family on a regular basis. They tend to get better grades and improve their language and literacy skills, are less likely to get entangled in addictions, and have less risk of obesity. Engaging in conversation builds their vocabulary and emotional intelligence. A daily time together allows parents to check on their emotional and physical health.[2]

This one was hard for us in certain seasons, especially soccer and volleyball season. The other challenge was my husband's career as a Realtor. Often, clients wanted to look at homes after their workday—which meant in the evening. So sometimes our family meals did not include my husband. I didn't let that imperfection stop me. The three of us would gather around the table, even if dinner was mac and cheese or reheated leftovers or scrambled eggs. While I wanted healthy, simple meals, the thing that mattered more was the conversation. Hospitality to your kids means listening to them, even when they ramble on. If they had friends over, they welcomed them to stay and eat with us.

I did not make separate food for my kids. It's hard enough to get dinner on the table, let alone make two different meals. They ate what we ate, in very small portions. If your kids are small, start as soon as possible to include them in dinner and don't make something different (like chicken nuggets) for them. If they won't eat, that's fine. Just tell them when they get hungry they can finish what they left on their plate.

That said, I have always loved to cook. It's how I unwind at the end of a long day. After sitting at my desk all day, I love to stand at the stove, chopping, stirring, sautéing, sipping. However, cooking is one thing. Making two different meals is another. I chose not to even offer that option to my kids. Both my children have thanked me for it. They attribute our approach to meals as the reason they both have become good cooks who know how to put a simple meal on the table, and the reason they are both adventurous eaters unafraid to try new foods. They cook for friends, because they know the value of gathering people around the table, and they feel comfortable engaging in conversations. They learned these life skills by practicing them at our kitchen table.

## Hospitality Is Caught More Than Taught

Ban all phones and devices from the dinner table—including your own. You may have to turn them off or put them in another room. My kids would often catch my husband texting at the table and call him out on it. Make the dinner table a screen-free zone. Don't watch television or even listen to it in the background.

Use open-ended questions to start conversations. Even something as simple as "What was the highlight of your day?" can get kids talking. If your kids' friends join you, include them in the conversation. Try to avoid questions that can be answered yes or no or "Fine." Smile sweetly at them when they roll their eyes. Save difficult conversations about bad grades or a call from their teacher for another time. Use family meals as a time to build up the people you live with, encouraging and cheering them on.

We required good manners—saying "please" and "thank you"—and help with cleanup. It's really not too much, and when their friends came over, we expected the same. They had to ask to be excused from the table after eating, then put their plates and cups in the dishwasher. We started this when they were in preschool.

Family meals are harder if you live alone, but consider inviting a few of your neighbors or a friend to share a meal once a week or even once a month. Broaden your definition of family, and family meals become an adventure.

## Opening Your Home—to Teenagers?

After Melanie went off to college, Aaron was still home with us for two more years. Things got quieter, in some ways. His senior year, he asked if we could host house groups.

Our church is large. The high school youth group, in particular, is very large—about a thousand kids from a dozen high schools attend. After a large gathering for worship and teaching at church, they head to homes near their own neighborhoods, hosted by families with kids who attend the same high school they do. Each group meets in the same house every week, so hosting house groups is a commitment to have about forty to sixty teenagers in your house nearly every Sunday afternoon during the school year. Other parents sign up to bring food for lunch each week, but it gets served in your kitchen, again with the help of more volunteers.

I was secretly delighted by his request. I'd wanted to volunteer to host but didn't want to jump in front of my kids. It's a pretty big commitment of time and energy.

We told Aaron we'd love to host, but he needed to be a full participant. We expected him to lead by example in the group, and to participate in cleaning up the house before and after each meeting. We talked about leadership, about being the host who welcomes every single kid, not just the cool kids. We talked about loving and welcoming everyone.

He agreed, and we jumped into a messy, loud version of welcoming friends and strangers. Aaron stepped up to welcome everyone, to lead by example. It was fun to watch him grow closer to God by taking on this adventure. We welcomed kids in Jesus's name, and in so doing, ushered Jesus right into our home.

The group used nearly every room in our house, because after lunch, they'd split into small groups: a girls group and guys group each for freshmen, sophomores, juniors, and seniors. That's eight meeting spaces—in bedrooms, the office, the basement, the living room.

The kids would come in and dutifully take off their shoes (or wet boots in winter) and leave them on a tarp we placed on the floor of the foyer. It may sound weird, but I would see that maze of oversize sneakers and Toms and Ugg boots and even flip-flops, which filled my foyer, and it just made my heart happy. My home was full of kids learning how much God loved them, teenagers experiencing the joy of community. They were becoming, as my son described it, like a family to one another. And we got to be a small part of it by offering the space for it. It felt like a sacred calling, and I watched my son grow in his leadership abilities as well as his ability to connect deeply with friends. I saw his faith bloom.

House groups can be hard on a house. The house got a bit messy every week. Aaron definitely had to make good on his promise to help clean. The kids would take off their shoes, but then run out to the backyard in their socks, and come trooping back with dirty socks. We have old carpet, so it wasn't a big deal. It made me laugh. Like, really, kids? Thanks for taking off your shoes!

One day, the freshmen boys practiced flips onto a beanbag chair in the basement. Unexpectedly, though not surprisingly, one of them, Trent, put his foot right through the drywall. My husband and I came down to survey the damage. I looked at Trent, who hung his head sheepishly. "You've gotta tuck when you land, buddy," I said, smiling.

The group leader assured me, "The church has a small budget for this type of repair."

"Oh, that's okay," my husband said. "We'll pay for it. We already have extra drywall and tape. But Trent is going to come over and help us repair it."

"Really?" the leader asked.

"I am?" Trent said.

"Absolutely. Every kid should know how to repair drywall." Scot taught our kids to paint, repair drywall, and more while they were in grade school. To him, home repair skills are as essential as, say, shoe tying or learning to ride a bike. He's astonished when people don't know how to paint.

Trent did come over, handing us a heartfelt, handwritten note of apology. That day, he learned how to fix a hole in a wall. Scot supervised but made him cut out the jagged edges, fit in a piece of drywall to patch the hole, tape, spread drywall compound, and sand the spot until it was perfectly smooth, then come back a few days later to paint it. We told him he was always welcome in our home, no matter what. We praised his handiwork.

Trent's parents were surprised at our reaction, but they definitely supported our request to have Trent learn a vital home repair skill, and to make amends with a bit of hard work. You might think Trent would avoid house groups or be embarrassed. Just the opposite. He seemed to feel empowered. At the next house group, he proudly showed his friends how he'd repaired the wall. He was there every week, always greeting me enthusiastically. He also began helping his small group leader corral the other wild boys in his group. He had become invested. He had been loved in our home. He began to lead by example, to encourage other kids, and to remind them to be really careful when doing flips in the basement.

Sometimes, hospitality is giving people the opportunity to be loved but also to face the consequences of their choices. It's treating them like family, in every way.

## A Gift or a Practice?

Is hospitality a gift that some people have, or a moral imperative for all Jesus followers? Is it only for those who have big houses and a flair for entertaining?

I know Christians who say hospitality just isn't their gift, it isn't their thing. It can be inconvenient. It can be intrusive. Saying it's not your gift gives you an out. But is hospitality a gift or does it just mean loving others?

When I was growing up in a strongly evangelical church, I understood that some people had a gift for evangelism—like Billy Graham. Others of us might not be gifted in that area, but my tradition's interpretation of Jesus's instructions to his disciples to go and preach the gospel, to make disciples—"Go into all the world and make disciples"—meant that everyone was supposed to witness and lead people to Christ. That was a bit like leading a horse to water, it seemed to me. We each kept a copy of the Four Spiritual Laws in our wallet at all times, just in case. People in my evangelical culture would actually ask how many people you'd led to Christ. (You were supposed to keep track and always look for opportunities for conversations that might take a turn for the spiritual.)

Evangelism was both a gift, which I don't have, and a general requirement of all Christians.

If that is how evangelism works, why don't we see hospitality in the same way? Some people are gifted for it, but all believers need to find a way to engage in it somehow. Telling people about God's love for them is a means of loving them yourself. We're invited to it, whether or not we are specifically gifted at it. After all, Jesus's last words to his followers were to "go into all the world and preach the gospel" (Mark 16:15), and the Bible says to "always be prepared to give an answer to everyone who asks you to give the reason for the hope that you have" (1 Pet. 3:15).

I've been told numerous times I have a spiritual gift of hospitality. But when I read the Bible, I don't see hospitality listed among the spiritual gifts. It's a spiritual practice, and it's something that Jesus invites us to do, but it's not a gift. The lists of gifts in the Bible are not necessarily exhaustive, but still— since the Bible talks a lot about hospitality, you'd think it would have made at least one of the top-ten lists. Nope.

We've agreed spiritual practices are not ways to earn God's favor. Nor are practices ideas that we simply think about or philosophical positions we affirm. Rather, practices are actions we literally do with our bodies that form us spiritually. Practices are not the same as gifts, although our gifts may shape the practices we are drawn to, and help us to grow. Practices draw us into God space, invite us into intimacy.

By gift, I mean a divine enablement, given by the Holy

Spirit, to build up the body of believers. The two main passages that list the spiritual gifts are in Romans 12 and 1 Corinthians 12, and a few more are listed in Ephesians 4. They include things like prophesy, teaching, giving, wisdom, knowledge, healing, tongues, interpretations, and service, just to name a few.

The Bible doesn't mention hospitality as a gift specifically. It mentions serving, a broad category that may include, but not be limited to, hospitality. It does mention hospitality as something all of us should engage in; just as we are to love one another, we are to offer hospitality to one another. In fact, love for neighbors and hospitality are often linked in Scripture.

The invitation to extend hospitality is mentioned in the context of loving others. Some of us may be more comfortable with it than others, but we're all asked to practice it. Hospitality, in some passages, seems to be an expression of worship, because worship is more about serving than singing. The apostle Paul instructed believers, "Be devoted to one another in love. Honor one another above yourselves. Never be lacking in zeal, but keep your spiritual fervor, serving the Lord. Be joyful in hope, patient in affliction, faithful in prayer. Share with the Lord's people who are in need. Practice hospitality" (Rom. 12:10–13).

Offering hospitality shows Christ to people. It is closely linked to both worship and generosity. We share our bread with those in need of food, or of fellowship, not to earn God's favor but so that we might be transformed. Remember, the purpose of spiritual practices is not to get good at the practice. They shape us into people who are more like Jesus, and are more deeply connected to Jesus.

Hospitality is not about entertaining or perfectionism. It's about love, letting the love God's lavished on you spill over onto others. Jesus told his followers: "A new command I give you: Love one another. As I have loved you, so you must love one another. By this everyone will know that you are my disciples, if you love one another" (John 13:34–35).

When asked what was the most important commandment, Jesus replied, "'Love the Lord your God with all your heart and with all your soul and with all your mind.' This is the first and greatest commandment. And the second is like it: 'Love your neighbor as yourself.' All the Law and the Prophets hang on these two commandments" (Matt. 22:37–40).

Whether or not we're gifted at love, Jesus asks us to love. Other passages in the New Testament elaborate on what it means to love, including numerous verses that tell us to practice hospitality. Hospitality is often mentioned in the New Testament in the context of exhortations to love one another. It is a way of loving our neighbor as ourselves. The Bible repeatedly links love and hospitality. We're commanded to love, to show hospitality, to do good and share with others, to serve. This is not a multiple-choice menu, but practices interwoven, tied together. Love, lived out in hospitality and generosity, is one of the requirements for church leaders in the early church, which Paul mentioned to Timothy:

"If anyone wants to provide leadership in the church, good! But there are preconditions: A leader must be well-thought-of, committed to his wife, cool and collected, accessible, and *hospitable*. He must know what he's talking about, not be overfond of wine, not pushy but gentle, not thin-skinned, not money-hungry. He must handle his own affairs well, attentive to his own children and having their respect" (1 Tim. 3:1–4, MESSAGE; emphasis mine).

Peter wrote about love, hospitality, and service as interconnected obligations:

"Above all, love each other deeply, because love covers over a multitude of sins. Offer hospitality to one another without grumbling. Each of you should use whatever gift you have received to serve others, as faithful stewards of God's grace in its various forms. If anyone speaks, they should do so as one who speaks the very words of God. If anyone serves, they should do so with the strength God provides, so that in all things God may be praised through Jesus Christ" (1 Pet. 4:8–11, NIV).

The writer of Hebrews also ties these same themes together, adding in visiting people in prison as a form of hospitality:

"Keep on loving one another as brothers and sisters. Do not forget to show hospitality to strangers, for by so doing some people have shown hospitality to angels without knowing it. Continue to remember those in prison as if you were together with them in prison, and those who are mistreated as if you yourselves were suffering....And do not forget to do good and to share with others, for with such sacrifices God is pleased" (Heb. 13:1–3, 16).

In the original Greek, the word in each of these texts is *philóxenos*, which we simply translate as "hospitality" or "hospitable." The latter word describes someone who is generous to guests and a lover of hospitality. In Greek culture, hospitality was understood to mean welcoming not just friends but strangers.

We can practice hospitality everywhere we go. My daughter used to keep granola bars in her car so that when she saw someone begging at an intersection, she could offer them a bit of food, and look them in the eye—a moment of hospitality before the light turned green.

We can listen to a friend. Giving someone the space to tell their story, to be heard—even if you meet them at Starbucks or go on a walk with them—this is hospitality as well.

I wonder what it would look like to welcome people graciously on, say, Facebook or Twitter. I see a lot of Christians behaving in ways you could never describe as hospitable on social media. Frankly, I've seen myself behaving inhospitably online. For me, it's sometimes easier to take in a stranger in my home than to walk away from arguments on Facebook. I've got lots of room to grow in this one.

## The Sufficiency of Provision

In the previous chapter, I described one of Sabbath keeping's essential truths as this: "the sufficiency of God's provision, [and our response to that] generous provision with both trust and our own willingness to be generous—extravagantly so— to ourselves, and to the people around us. These two things:

trust of God, and generosity to neighbor, lie at the heart of the Sabbath."

The same could be said of hospitality. It, too, affirms trust of God and generosity to neighbor. It affirms that you have sufficient reserves to share. It says there is enough food on the table, enough space—even if it is on the couch or an air mattress.

To me, the ultimate story of hospitality is the story of the widow and Elijah. The widow would never be featured in Martha Stewart's magazine or anything close. But she chose to practice hospitality when it was hard. Here's her story:

Some time later the brook dried up because there had been no rain in the land. Then the word of the LORD came to him: "Go at once to Zarephath in the region of Sidon and stay there. I have directed a widow there to supply you with food." So he went to Zarephath. When he came to the town gate, a widow was there gathering sticks. He called to her and asked, "Would you bring me a little water in a jar so I may have a drink?" As she was going to get it, he called, "And bring me, please, a piece of bread."

"As surely as the LORD your God lives," she replied, "I don't have any bread—only a handful of flour in a jar and a little olive oil in a jug. I am gathering a few sticks to take home and make a meal for myself and my son, that we may eat it—and die."

Elijah said to her, "Don't be afraid. Go home and do as you have said. But first make a small loaf of bread for me from what you have and bring it to me, and then make something for yourself and your son. For this is what the LORD, the God of Israel, says: 'The jar of flour will not be used up and the jug of oil will not run dry until the day the LORD sends rain on the land.'"

She went away and did as Elijah had told her. So there was food every day for Elijah and for the woman and her family. For the jar of flour was not used up and the jug of oil did not run dry, in keeping with the word of the LORD spoken by Elijah. (1 Kings 17:7–16)

Like so many women of the Bible, we don't know her name: she's just a widow. The Bible labels her "the widow of Zarephath," after the place where she lives. God tells Elijah that he's directed the widow to feed him, but their initial conversation sounds like she didn't get the memo about that.

Zarephath, scholars tell us, was known as a place where the main industry was the "refining and smelting of metals."[3] Think Pittsburgh, Pennsylvania, or Gary, Indiana, in their steel-factory heydays. It's a wonderful detail that we might overlook, how a woman living in a town known for refining would have her own faith tested and strengthened by the fire of an inconvenient request. How fitting that in a place where ore was transformed into precious metal, a bit of flour and the last few drops of oil were miraculously turned into three years' worth of provision.

Elijah comes during a famine, and asks her to provide him with hospitality: a simple meal of bread and water. Martha Stewart, or even Martha of Bethany, she is not. "I'm getting ready to eat and die," she says, implying that she might wish the same fate on this demanding prophet.

But she is invited to trust. Elijah calmly challenges her to take a chance on divine provision. In essence, the prophet promises a miracle. There will be enough, if you are generous. If you are not generous, your prediction of this meal being your last may be accurate. If you give to God first (he asks that she make him a loaf of bread, then make one for herself and her son), God will provide.

It's not a threat. It's a promise. Trust, and watch what God will do. Note that Elijah doesn't demand to be fed instead of her son, but only to share what they have.

In the same way, the practice of hospitality invites us to trust, to pull up another chair to the table and share a modest meal. The widow made bread of flour and olive oil, served with water. She set the bar for biblical hospitality pretty low, with regard to the food. But she set it pretty high for trust, considering that she kept on giving what she thought was the very last of her provisions.

What went through that widow's heart during that first meal with Elijah? And what happened when she went back to the jar the next day, and shook out another portion of flour? Then poured out a few more squirts of oil? And the next day, and the next? Surely, her amazement and wonder grew each day. But each day, did she think, This is it; this is where God's provision ends? Did she doubt?

We'd understand if she did, right? But whether she doubted isn't mentioned. If she did doubt, she wasn't punished for that. Despite her doubt, she acted. She made the bread—embodying her faith by pouring out oil, kneading bread, handing it to Elijah, then her son. Sometimes we doubt, and that's understandable and okay. But when we risk obedience, our risk is rewarded. We get to experience doubt-dispelling miracles that we'd never get to see if we hadn't taken that chance.

What would it look like for you to follow the example of this widow? To be generous not out of your abundance but out of what you've got? Generosity and hospitality, in divine alchemy, turn scarcity into abundance.

## Not Entertaining

Hospitality is not entertaining. It's a way of inviting people into God space. It invites them into a Sabbath space—no matter which day of the week they visit. Hospitality provides friends or strangers a place to rest, to put their feet up and be refreshed. It invites them to trust God—because through you, God provides for and feeds them.

When we engage in the practice of hospitality, we invite people to slow down, to linger over dinner, to sip and savor. Imagine gathering friends for dinner, then telling them, "Glad you could make it, but you'll need to eat quickly because I have plans for later this evening."

No. When we welcome people to our home or our table, when we go to the trouble of preparing a meal, even a simple one, we want them to enjoy it. We want them to appreciate it. It's hard to appreciate in a hurry. In fact, that's why a leisurely meal is such a gift: it's so rare these days.

Saying yes to opportunities to extend the grace of hospital-ity doesn't just show God's love to the person who comes to my home. It allows *me* to experience love, and the presence of God—just as I might when I engage in prayer, or worship, or when I watch a beautiful sunset. I feel God when I feed people, when I love them by creating a space for them in my home. At my table, I want to not just say grace, but extend it. Grace is when you expect the minimum and receive more than you'd ever expect.

As long as we view hospitality as entertaining, as a way for us to show off or impress or get what we're craving, it will be a chore. We'll feel put upon, even resentful. It will make us anxious. But when we view it as a way of creating space for God in our own life, it becomes a spiritual practice. And like any spiritual practice, perfectionism destroys it. Expecting people to be impressed will wreck it. Pouting if they don't praise you will hinder whatever God's trying to do in you through hospitality. Worrying about the meal's imperfections or the shabby carpeting is missing the point. Gently loosen your grip on perfectionism. Just as you don't need to try to become an expert at solitude or an Olympic level prayer warrior, achievement is not your aim with hospitality. The goal of any practice is greater intimacy with God—which feels sometimes like joy, or a sense of divine purpose.

A strange delight wells up in me when people are around the table, when everyone feels cared for and nurtured and well fed, and relishes the conversation. I love a table full of food and an interesting mix of people who are not in a hurry, invited to engage and feast on conversation. I'm not impressing people with my mad cooking skills. When they experience being loved and welcomed at the table, the joy it brings me is visceral. To facilitate a good meal, good conversation is deeply satisfying to me. To know that people experience love in my home, because of a meal or a comfortable bed or restful space, is a gift I receive when I give space, time, a meal.

If the idea of cooking for others stresses you out, be assured that cooking is not the main point. Get carryout or prepared stuff. Focus less on the food and more on welcoming people, having a ministry of presence. Ask good questions. Listen well. Put away phones and all devices, and invite people into simple conversation. Ask people to share their stories and connect in meaningful ways. If that seems like a stretch, start small. The question: "Where have you noticed God lately?" can be an amazing conversation opener.

When we gather people at my table, I want them to be fed, not just physically but spiritually. I want them to feel safe and satisfied. I want them to be welcomed as if they were Jesus, and in that welcoming, experience for themselves the presence and sustenance of God.

Offering hospitality means taking a risk. It goes so far beyond entertaining—in fact, it is altogether different. Entertaining is offered with the assumption that those invited will return the favor. Its focus is on impressing others, earning favor. Hospitality, in the Bible, was offered not just to friends but to strangers. There was an obligation, in that ancient culture, to provide hospitality to travelers. Pastor and scholar Ray Vander Laan explains:

Survival in the desert literally demands that its people care for one another. Even today, Bedouin will say that the unbelievable commitment to hospitality expressed among desert tribes exists in part because as they travel through the barren wilderness they need to depend on others for food, shelter, and especially water. So the code of hospitality is very strong.

In the desert, guests and complete strangers are welcomed and receive the best food and water a family has. Families will serve the last bit of flour they have or defend a guest in their tent with their lives—even if they just met that guest. This code of hospitality is quite foreign to many people in the Western world where privacy, competition, and a spirit of self-sufficiency prevail.

Perhaps it shouldn't surprise us that God chose the desert to be the place where he would prepare his people to be his community of priests who would reveal him to the world.[4]

You probably don't live in the desert. Strangers may not walk up and knock on your door, asking for a place to stay and a bottle of water. But what if Jesus's followers, you and I, decided to redefine the practice of hospitality according to its biblical roots? What if we decided to unpin hospitality from Pinterest, to help people understand the difference between hospitality and entertaining, to make it countercultural? Since the Bible talks so much about hospitality, what if Jesus followers were known for *that* instead of being known for what we're against? What if we gave people, even those far from God, a chance to experience intimacy with God by gathering around a table and sharing their stories?

Engage this practice by starting where you are. If you live with other people, show hospitality to them by sharing meals. If you live alone, invite someone to your home, or even out to coffee. Offer the ministry of presence, of listening.

Do you know your neighbors? If not, go introduce yourself. You don't have to invite them to dinner, just meet them. That's a great first step.

If you've never opened your home, pray bravely about this practice. What would that look like in your context? What next step of hospitality is God inviting you to take?

The Bible says that this serving of one another is not just hospitality, but our "spiritual worship." We'll explore the adventure of that kind of worship in the next chapter.

# Worship

## *Space in the World*

At the funeral, there's standing room only downstairs. Scot and I climb the red-carpeted stairs and slip into the first pew of the balcony. Incense, redolent, tickles my nose, imparts solemnity and mystery. The powder-blue ceiling, arched, hung with gilded chandeliers, evokes a faded spring sky.

The singing rising from below, though I can't understand the words, communicates crystal clear a quiet reverence. The strong voices fill the space—mournful yet full of a quiet confidence, beseeching yet faithful. I see my friend Liza in the front row, next to her daughter, Tamar, who is one of my daughter's best friends. Liza's husband, Armen, listens as the priest eulogizes his father.

The priest, in a black hood and ornate gold-and-black cape, holds a scepter in one hand and a small white handkerchief in the other. He begins speaking in Armenian as he stands before an elaborately draped casket. Though I can't understand the words, I recognize names when the priest speaks them. I'm moved by the passion in his voice.

Tamar, the oldest grandchild, walks to a crimson-draped

podium to share some memories about her Baba. As always, she is wise and funny and articulate—and speaking, thankfully, in English. She flew home from Taiwan, where she's on a Fulbright scholarship, to be with her family for her grandfather's funeral.

The service resumes in Armenian, prayers sung, words spoken. While I intellectually understood only a portion of the service, I *understood* all of it on another level. The church was full of love and respect. The service was saturated with worship for a God who helped the Armenian community survive a holocaust, who has held them together. I understood that this community worships a God who did not prevent calamity, but is faithful nonetheless; a God who cannot be manipulated, and is therefore revered. The worship was palpable without being overly emotional. I prayed for my friends, for their heavy hearts. I gave attention to what God was doing in that room. When people prayed, I simply told God "what they said." When the priest spoke, my soul whispered, "Amen," trusting that was enough.

My Armenian friends help me understand the meaning of community. In fact, they refer to their church and friends as "the community." Life has struggles—this they well know. And yet, they experience God's presence in the presence of one another, and in the traditions, prayers, and incense and the arched blue ceilings of a little church.

## The Power of Awe

I grew up in Chicago, but once my brother and I were out of the house, my parents packed up and moved to San Diego. It's hard to be far away from them, but San Diego is a pretty great place to visit. I spend as much time there as I can—especially because my daughter chose to go to college in Los Angeles and still lives there.

A few Christmases ago, my gift to our family was a day of sea kayaking. We go to San Diego to visit my parents at Christmas, and I was looking for something a bit more interesting for my teenagers than going to the San Diego Zoo, since they've been going there almost every year since they were toddlers.

A few months before that, I'd told my adventurous, outdoorsy daughter about wanting to go sea kayaking myself, and she had been skeptical. "I don't know if you'll do that," she said. One of her part-time jobs in college was to lead kayaking and backpacking trips as a guide. Game on, I told her. That Christmas, the four of us found ourselves paddling across the bay in La Jolla with a group of other tourists and a couple of guides.

Our hope was to see some of the gray whales migrating down the California coast from Alaska to Mexico. As we paddled, we saw California sea lions, seagulls, even dolphins. Suddenly our guide said, "Paddle hard this way! Gray whales out ahead."

We all paddled as hard as we could and headed toward the open sea. I strained my eyes where they pointed, seeing nothing but ocean. We paddled more against the gentle surf.

Suddenly our guide held a hand up, and we watched the open water where he'd pointed. Not far from our kayak I saw a gray whale break the surface of the bay, exhaling a sigh of mist and seawater, then slip in a hulking gray curve back under the water.

Even my jaded teenagers later said, "That was pretty cool."

We all felt a sense of awe watching these giant creatures swim past. Seeing a whale at eye level from a kayak. Staring up at a star-studded night sky from a place where you can actually see those stars, and peering through a telescope to see the Andromeda galaxy—the galaxy next door! Hiking in Bryce Canyon and Arches National Park in Utah. Watching the Joffrey Ballet perform. These experiences have brought me moments of awe.

Scientists are now studying awe as an emotion, and discovering that we are wired for awe. It is definitely a God space emotion. Awe causes us to stop in our tracks, to consider something outside of ourselves. Psychologists exploring the emotion say that it occurs when we encounter something vast, bigger than ourselves, transcendent, that we realize we can't fully understand. In recognizing our smallness, we experience a collision of joy, reverence, and even a little fear. It's a feeling of "Whoaaaa!"

Scientists are discovering that human beings need awe for optimal functioning. We need it! Awe makes us slow down, stop, reflect. In that awed state, we are more open to new ideas and even transformation. Awe makes us healthier humans. It feeds our minds and souls. We are wired for awe, because God made us, and desires connection with us. Through the beauty, splendor, and sheer awesomeness of creation, God reaches toward us, hoping to stop us in our tracks, to get us to connect and reflect and, yes, to worship.

But it is one thing to feel awe when we see something spectacular in nature or hear a moving piece of music. It's another to make a regular practice of worship. Opening ourselves and our lives to awe can lead us to worship.

Have you considered deliberately putting yourself into situations where you will feel awe, as an exercise for your soul? Get out and look at the night sky. Stand on the shore of the ocean. Look at a mountain. If you live in the Midwest like I do, watch movies of mountains and oceans. Just kidding. Opportunities for awe abound even in not-so-scenic places. Right now, the fall colors are blazing around my neighborhood. I keep telling myself to slow down and just look at the beauty, to be awed by the annual miracle of maple leaves. I make myself step outside the back door at sunrise and look at the sky and trees and sun filtering through them and allow myself a few moments of wonder.

Worship is not slavish, blind, sycophantic. When we worship, we give God glory. We honor, exalt, revere. We take our eyes, attention, and concern off of ourselves, and focus on God's amazing, awe-inspiring power, strength, tenderness, love. God is vast beyond us, yet desires to be our intimate friend. This, in itself, is awe-inspiring.

## How Do We Worship?

Worship recalibrates our hearts, giving us a right-sized view of ourselves, particularly in relation to God. Ideally, it removes us, along with our worries, fears, and ambitions, from the throne of our lives and puts God back on it. It creates space amidst the strife, conflict, and all the things that God is not, so we can focus on God.

Worship is about bringing a sacrifice to God, giving to God. God is worthy of worship, and he asks us to have no other gods. The Almighty asks for our worship.

John Ortberg writes,

So why does God insist on our worship? Does he really need to have a whole planet full of creatures spending vast amounts of effort and time dreaming up ways to tell him how great he is? Doesn't he already know that?

Worship is not about filling God's unmet ego needs. God has made us so that when we experience something transcendentally great, we have a need to praise it. Our experience is incomplete until we can wrap words around it. When we see the Grand Tetons for the first time, a double rainbow, or a nest of baby herons getting ready for their first flight, something in our spirits demands that we express the joy we receive."[1]

Worship is awe, expressed, acknowledging God.

We tend to make worship, especially of the musical variety, about us. "What a great worship time we had in church today," we say, as if we were attending a concert or show. We judge how good the worship (meaning music and singing) is by how it moves us, how it stirs up all the feelings for us, how it moves us to raise our hands and cry a little.

I am part of a church that celebrates and worships with excellence, creativity, and exuberance, from singing, spoken word, dance, and instrumental music, all of it very professional and polished, but absolutely heartfelt as well. But if my definition of worship is a certain genre of music, I'm missing out on opportunities for intimacy with God, opportunities for spiritual transformation. It's easier to just listen, or even sing along, and let worship sweep me away. It's less convenient to do the hard work of offering my body as a living sacrifice and engaging in what we might more readily label service. But the Bible equates service—using our gifts to serve others—with worship.

The Bible certainly encourages us to "sing to the Lord" and to "make a joyful noise" but that's only one small part of worship.

It is tragic when we make worship an experience in which we feel moved or satisfied. We judge its worth by how it stirs our emotions. Worship has become tainted by our consumer mind-set; we will stroll out of church without a touch of irony saying, "Wow, that was such great worship," as if we're describing a great meal at a restaurant, or a clickbait video on Facebook.

Maybe modern-day worship music can get in the way of actually worshipping God. It's become a genre, an industry. Although this industry is slipping in influence from its heyday in the 1990s, it still feels more about record sales and creating superstars than honoring God.

"When the mind is disengaged and worship is reduced to an emotional experience, worship descends into narcissistic and self-referential meaninglessness,' Jonathan Aigner wrote in a blog post titled "8 Reasons the Worship Industry Is Killing Worship."[2]

We can worship God by singing, but I don't think watching other people perform music is necessarily worship.

Certainly, we can be inspired and even awed by hearing someone sing well. Their lyrics can express for us the things we would say to God; they can put words to the longing within us to connect. I enjoy a variety of worship music, from hymns to modern choruses, even classical. Mozart or Vivaldi or Handel speak to my soul of God, without words. However, worship is meant to be part of our embodied spirituality. It's what we do.

I'm not talking about raising your arms during the singing. Worship is what we do for God, actions that take us out of ourselves, redirect our focus. In losing ourselves, we find our meaning, connection that leads us to awe, reverence, and intimacy with God.

If we come at worship seeking an experience, demanding intimacy, wanting to be moved emotionally, we will settle for that. However, worship, throughout the recorded history of our faith, is embodied spirituality. That means faith integrated with action. Worship requires us to integrate contemplation and action. Worship is not just what we say or believe. Worship is not only action. It is both, together.

In ancient days, this often meant engaging in a ritual: building a pile of stones, walking through a flock, selecting a perfect lamb, bringing it to the altar, slitting its throat, lighting a fire, smelling the roasting meat. In rituals, those bodily actions, God's people experienced moments of reflection and repentance, gratitude, and even celebration. In that culture, killing an animal was a financial sacrifice as well—to give part of your provision or inventory to God. In a beautiful picture of how God gives back to us, the people were sometimes instructed to sacrifice an animal, but then to eat it, or to share it.

What is it that I do today to sacrifice? Not as they did in ancient days, because Jesus took care of that once and for all. What if I need to sacrifice my privilege, my convenience?

## Prayers, Spoken or Sung (or Lived)

The first question of the Westminster Shorter Catechism asks, "What is the chief end of man?" The answer: "Man's chief end is to glorify God, and to enjoy him forever."[3]

The old-fashioned (gender exclusive—sorry!) language really asks, "Why are we here? What's the meaning and purpose of human existence?" The answer, at least in 1646, was "to glorify and enjoy God." It's still the reason we're here, but something we've lost sight of in our busy, hurried, crowded lives.

Rick Warren put it more succinctly: the purpose of your life is "not about you."

Our purpose is to glorify God. Conversely, it is in fulfilling our life purpose that we do glorify God. We glorify God with our words and our actions. And in that we find joy. We enjoy God. Worship is enjoying God.

There's a big difference between enjoying God and being entertained by worship music. While worship is more than singing, more than music, it can be an appropriate accompaniment to worship in action. I'm cynical about the industry of Christian music, yet songs have offered me a sound track to moments of worship. In those moments, actions and music collided and brought me closer to Jesus in unexpected ways. But those unexpected worship moments happened when I took myself out into the world and lived my faith.

When Aaron was a senior in high school, he and I spent part of his spring break on a mission trip to Chicago with the high school ministry from our suburban church. I was a team leader, meaning I was both driver and chaperone for a team of kids. I drove a twelve-passenger van loaded with kids down the Dan Ryan Expressway to the south side of Chicago, where we slept on the floor of the huge sanctuary at Salem Baptist Church, and drove them to places like Union Gospel Mission during the day. I earned the respect of the kids on my team, not only by driving on the Dan Ryan, but also parallel parking the van on a city street in one try. We worshipped with our hands and feet, serving meals or making beds or doing whatever tasks the ministries we visited asked us to do.

One shelter we visited was an apartment building for women fleeing violence of the streets or their own homes. My team first helped paint some walls in a common area, then was assigned to clean an apartment that had been left in disarray when a tenant abandoned the program. Everything was grimy, from the walls and stove top to the utensils and pots and pans. Ten high school kids and I cleaned up the entire apartment to ready it for a new tenant. The kids remained amazingly cheerful about this task. I will never forget washing dishes and scrubbing walls (there's that embodied spirituality) alongside these teens, who as they cleaned, began singing worship choruses.

Out of their comfort zone, these suburban kids trusted God and worshipped not just by singing but also by obeying that call from God to bless the poor, to serve with their hands and feet. They'd given up part of their spring break to do grunt work in shelters and sleep on a church floor. They trusted that scrubbing grease off the walls of an inner-city apartment was actually a way to worship. They believed with action and truth that in the neighborhoods of the south side of Chicago, they might have been out of their depth, but they walked brave and sang loud, the melody transforming the space we found ourselves in.

It was a holy moment.

In another, completely different setting, I remember driving into Arches National Park with my daughter as the sun was coming up. We were trekking across the country to take her to college, stopping at several national parks in Utah on our way to California. Melanie queued up Matt Redmon's song "10,000 Reasons" on her phone, and as the morning light lit up the curious and beautiful landscape, we sang along.

It's a crystallized memory, a moment of bittersweet awe that made my eyes sting a bit—launching my firstborn child into the world felt much like the edge of the wilderness, uncharted as the land we drove through. Could I still be singing, even as my child moved two thousand miles away from home? Did I trust God to take care of her, to guide her, to be present with her when I was not? Was I willing to let go of my illusions of control? Could I live the trust I sang about?

Our worship that day was to walk among those otherworldly rock formations and canyons, marveling at the work of the Creator. And to realize that the God who made our amazing planet was also mindful of us, his tiny, frail, fallible creatures.

Worship happens in the city, in the wilderness, even in the suburbs, when we get outside of ourselves and focus on God. We cannot manufacture "enjoyment of God," but it comes when we let go of our self-absorption and needs, and give glory to whom it's due.

"There are numerous definitions of the word *worship*. Yet,

one in particular encapsulates the priority we should give to worship as a spiritual discipline: *Worship is to honor with extravagant love and extreme submission* (Webster's Dictionary, 1828)," wrote Delesslyn A. Kennebrew in an article for ChristianityToday.com. "True worship, in other words, is defined by the priority we place on *who* God is in our lives and *where* God is on our list of priorities.... Worship is having an extravagant or exaggerated love for God."[4]

## Just Not Feeling It

But what to do if we're just not feeling it? How do you manufacture an "exaggerated love for God"?

It's not something you can fake, however, it is something you can decide to cultivate. For me, that happens when I get out of the pew and into the world and do. When I serve the poor or hike through a national park, listen to someone who just needs to talk and cry. Like our ability to run or work out, worship gets stronger with repetition. That's why we call spiritual practices "disciplines."

Scientists who study the emotion of awe actually recommend seeking out awe-inducing experiences. They might not call it that, but they're inviting all of us into spiritual disciplines. Go look at the night sky. Take time to notice things vast and beautiful. Consider the creation. Look at, contemplate, think about. Walk your body outside and just breathe in the air, open your eyes to see the light, notice beauty. As the Psalmist writes,

Lord, our Lord,
> how majestic is your name in all the earth!
> You have set your glory
> in the heavens.
Through the praise of children and infants
> you have established a stronghold against your
> enemies,
> to silence the foe and the avenger.
**When I consider** your heavens,
> the work of your fingers,
> the moon and the stars,
> which you have set in place,
what is mankind that you are mindful of them,
> human beings that you care for them? (Ps. 8:1–4,
> emphasis mine)

By exposing ourselves regularly to the creation, to God's work in the world, to beauty, we can move our hearts to worship. By regularly choosing to notice and name God's work in the world, we will build worship reflexes, adoration muscles. Worship begins when we slow our pace and really consider who God is, the wonder of creation and the power that sustains it.

I live in the Chicago suburbs, home to strip malls and subdivisions, but also farm fields and forest preserves—swaths of woodland set aside long ago as natural areas protected from development. While it is not a place known for its scenery, I find it beautiful at times—when the sun slips through the fall colors to light up the woods, or a quiet snowfall coats every bare branch in my backyard like frosting. But opportunities to experience awe don't come across my path all that often.

This may sound silly, but I follow accounts like NatGeo (National Geographic) and NASA on Instagram. Their photos of polar bears, mountains, nebulae in space, make me pause and wonder at the beauty of the world. It's especially helpful when much of social media is tangled in arguments and bogged down in strife. I also make it a regular practice to get outside. I may not live in the mountains or at the seashore, but the prairies and forests of the Midwest are full of beauty; you need only get out in them and take a look. For me, spending time outside every day is essential to both my physical and spiritual health. Whenever possible, I run on the trails of a local forest preserve.

Look for beauty around you, even in the ordinary. Choose to see what is right in front of you: your children in those rare moments when they are sweet and snuggly, a single fallen leaf, the bird building a nest outside your window, the gold and blue of the sunset. Stop, breathe, invite yourself to feel awe, and consciously choose to worship. Give yourself some space to enjoy God. Create some God space by slowing down enough to notice and acknowledge and consider the work of God's fingers, and also to personalize the question of the Psalm: Who am I that you are mindful of me, God?

## Let My People Go

Worship is not always convenient, especially when we're feeling disappointed with God, or experiencing pain. Sometimes,

I just do not feel worship-y. I'd rather file a complaint with God's customer service department.

God invites us into intimacy born of trust. And trust sometimes is built when we do what is hard. When we worship in the midst of our pain, when we focus on God instead of ourselves, we might experience something unexpected.

In the Old Testament account of the Israelites' exodus from slavery in Egypt, Moses repeatedly asks Pharaoh, "Let my people go, so that they may worship me." It's interesting that the songs I grew up singing in church left out the second part of that sentence. It was just "let my people go!" The implication was because they were oppressed, they were slaves, and they didn't want to be slaves. They wanted freedom. But freedom to do what? According to the text, they wanted to worship.

Moses's campaign for freedom begins with a request for a long weekend off—a three-day festival in the desert. Maybe he spun it as something similar to the Wild Goose Festival. (That part is not in the Bible.) The text actually says,

> Moses and Aaron went to Pharaoh and said, "This is what the LORD, the God of Israel, says: 'Let my people go, so that they may hold a festival to me in the wilderness.'"
>
> Pharaoh said, "Who is the LORD, that I should obey him and let Israel go? I do not know the LORD and I will not let Israel go."
>
> Then they said, "The God of the Hebrews has met with us. Now let us take a three-day journey into the wilderness to offer sacrifices to the LORD our God, or he may strike us with plagues or with the sword." (Exod. 5:1–3)

Pharaoh scoffs and says he does not know their God, and is not interested in losing his labor force. And in fact, he makes their work harder and things get worse before they get better. Moses is bummed, to put it mildly. *Bummed* is not in the Bible, but read Exodus; Moses does file an honest complaint with God.

From there, the story grows increasingly fascinating and terrifying. Pharaoh eventually begins to be worn down by the plagues that God keeps bringing: frogs that show up and then die in stinky piles, flies, the list goes on. After the eighth plague (locusts), Moses, with his trusty sidekick, Aaron, goes back to Pharaoh and repeats his request, again asking to be let go *so that they can worship*. Pharaoh appears to be caving, however slowly. He makes desperate attempts to hold on to control, but you can see he's crumbling as Moses gains confidence. Frog and locust warfare will do that. The text says,

> Then Moses and Aaron were brought back to Pharaoh. "Go, worship the LORD your God," he said. "But tell me who will be going."
>
> Moses answered, "We will go with our young and our old, with our sons and our daughters, and with our flocks and herds, because we are to celebrate a festival to the LORD." (Exod. 10:8–9)

Pharaoh bargains with Moses and Aaron and says that *just the men* can go to worship, ostensibly, just for a short time. Moses refuses, saying that the women and children, and all the animals, need to come along. Pharaoh says no, and the next plague (darkness) soon descends.

Moses goes back again and repeats his demand: *Let my people go, so that we can worship the Lord.* And Pharaoh, trying to get the plagues to stop, says, *Okay, fine, the women and children can go, too—but not the animals.* Moses bravely holds his ground.

> But Moses said, "You must allow us to have sacrifices and burnt offerings to present to the LORD our God. Our livestock too must go with us; not a hoof is to be left behind. We have to use some of them in worshiping the LORD our God, and until we get there we will not know what we are to use to worship the LORD." (Exod. 10:25–26)

Moses says, *I need to bring the cows and the sheep and all that, because I'm not sure which one God will want us to sacrifice.* Moses's negotiations are almost comical. Pharaoh basically says no way. So Moses says, *Get ready, you'll be sorry.* Before the final plague, in which the firstborn of every household will be killed, God instructs Moses about the Passover. A lamb sacrificed, its blood spread on the doorposts. What a beautiful visual foreshadowing of Christ on the cross. The homes with the blood painted on the door frame would be "passed over" and spared death.

That worship required actions, done with their bodies— each family chose a lamb, then slaughtered and roasted it. Imagine it: a branch of hyssop, dipped in the slaughtered lamb's blood and brushed on the lintel; the doorposts red and dripping. With their hands they made bread without yeast, then sat down and ate the bread and roasted lamb. God's people worshipped in that moment not by thinking good thoughts about God, or singing, but by doing, even by eating. They experienced "embodied spirituality."

This happened not after God had freed them, but *before*. There's a quiet irony in the story. Moses asks Pharaoh to let his people go *so that* they can worship. But they worship right there, in Egypt, waiting for the word to flee for their freedom— and possibly not sure that they will get it. They worship while they're still in slavery, when things are still a mess, when their pain is unresolved, when they're facing a Pharaoh who has so far been unmoved by nine horrific plagues.

God spells out an order of worship, of Passover, steeped in symbolism that they don't yet understand. In that first Passover, God allows them to practice how they will worship for generations to come. While things still look bleak, God asks them to worship.

They don't need to go to the wilderness to worship. They worship right where they are, before their pain is resolved. They learn the liturgy right there, under Pharaoh's nose, *before* they are free. And then they flee, taking their freedom, and God goes before them and with them.

When we worship, even in captivity, we experience freedom. We can worship right where we are, even if we feel hopeless, enslaved, exhausted. The intimacy we seek with God comes when we worship, even in the midst of our pain and unresolved problems.

## A Living Sacrifice

Worship, according to the Bible, is offering sacrifices—the very thing Moses asked Pharaoh to let him take the Israelites out into the wilderness to do. Since Jesus was sacrificed once for all, we have a new approach to God, but worship still involves sacrifice: actions taken, at a personal cost to ourselves. To sacrifice an animal required giving up something, being generous with resources. Although we don't have to sacrifice animals any longer, God still invites us to embrace the inconvenience of sacrifice, asks us to let go of a few of our resources: time, money, even ambition or self-absorption.

The apostle Paul urged an embodied spirituality when he wrote to the church at Rome: "Therefore, I urge you, brothers and sisters, in view of God's mercy, to offer your bodies as a living sacrifice, holy and pleasing to God—this is your true and proper worship. Do not conform to the pattern of this world, but be transformed by the renewing of your mind. Then you will be able to test and approve what God's will is— his good, pleasing and perfect will" (Rom. 12:1–2).

Animal sacrifice, among both Jews and pagans, was still common practice when Paul wrote his letter to the church at Rome. One commentary notes, "A living sacrifice, however, is a contradiction in terms. A believer is to be a living sacrifice, one who turns her mind completely to the will of God and thus knows what is good and perfect in God's sight. Part of being a living sacrifice and renewing one's mind is recognizing soberly one's talents and abilities as given by God."[5]

And, I would add, putting those talents and abilities to work for the good of others. This is where transformation happens.

Paul's exhortation to offer a "living sacrifice" must have prompted some interesting discussions as the early church read through his letter. What did that mean? Sacrifice of an animal, of course, means that the animal is not living, but killed. Our current worship practice does not include animal sacrifice (read the book of Hebrews for more on this) but something has to die when we worship. Our self, or more specifically our false self, has to die.

The false self is the one we put out in front of people most of the time. It is the inauthentic image that we try to project to look powerful or important. We use our false self to protect ourselves, but ironically, our false self is based on shame and weakness. The text says you'll be "transformed by the renewing of your mind." Think differently, think new thoughts, clear ones, about your false self, and you'll be changed.

Worship can help us shed that false self, to find our authentic self. It will lead us not to self-loathing but a right-sized view of ourselves. We rejoice in being a child of God, cared for, protected, safe. Worship invites us to trust, to grab hold of the life that is truly life.

Paul elaborates by writing about spiritual gifts, and exhorts us to know and exercise our gifts. Serving in our area of giftedness is a form of worship.

When I serve and use my gifts, I find myself in a God space. I may show up reluctantly, but as I serve, I begin to let go of myself, and I experience joy. God gives me words, on the page or as I speak, that encourage and strengthen others and, oddly enough, me. I shed the burden of my false self. At first that feels risky and frighteningly vulnerable, but ultimately it brings me a deep sense of contentment and peace.

One of the ways I worship is to serve at my church. Over the years, I've done everything from writing to child care to teaching to leading small groups.

People often wonder how our church got so large and sustains its growth. The secret is not innovative programming or excellent teaching, though we certainly have those things. The key is the value of serving. If you call Willow Creek Community Church home, eventually, you serve somewhere. Everyone contributes to the life of the body. Everyone feels as though they make an essential contribution—because they do.

My kids volunteered as soon as they were old enough. My daughter led a small group in the three-year-old room and volunteered at our church food pantry. My son was a small group leader in the junior high ministry and helped lead a student-worship gathering at his high school.

For many years, our serving was done in our home, hosting house groups and international guests, as I discussed in the previous chapter.

After both kids left for college, I felt a bit unmoored. Where did I fit now? The student ministry asked me to lead a group, but that didn't seem like the right place for me. It had been a few years since I'd taught classes, and I didn't really feel like it was time to go back to that. I asked God to show me where I should go next. I was open to anything, really.

Because of an unexpected invitation that came quite soon after that prayer, I now serve as a response pastor at our church. As the name implies, our team responds to people who need a pastor. We listen, pray with people, provide counseling referrals, and more. Many times, we are first responders for people in crisis. Most of the time, we work over the phone, as our church gets calls from not only members but the general public. We also meet with people who stop by our care center and need someone to listen and pray, along with a bag of groceries.

Volunteering in this way has been surprisingly fulfilling. I did not expect to be able to do this. I feel God has kindly given me the ability to do it.

## Paying Attention

A few years ago, I wrote this about a night at church when God gently upended my definition of worship:

> I slip into the aisle, too late realizing that the man and woman at the end of the row, whom I must step over awkwardly, are huddled in a miserable side-by-side embrace. Her head is bowed, obviously with grief. We slide past them to the empty seats, then begin to sing. It's hard for me to get into it; I almost didn't want to come to church tonight. I'm mad at Scot about something, I can't remember what, exactly.
>
> I sing mechanically. The woman now to our right continues to cry, her head down, the man beside her continues with his arm protectively around her. It's a little annoying. She's distracting.
>
> A few moments later, it dawns on me: maybe I'm not just here for me, tonight. I wonder what would happen if I let go of my annoyance, and just prayed for this woman. Since that's not something I would typically come up with on my own, I decide that might be God, asking me to make some space.
>
> I would like to hang on to my annoyance, my own stuff. Reluctantly at first, I pay attention to God's whispers, and

start to pray for the crying woman. I pray that the singing around her will soothe her soul, that God will heal her grief. I wonder what she's lost; I can tell it's that kind of grief.

After a while, the woman in front of this girl turns to her and hands her an entire packet of tissues. She takes them wordlessly, nods her thanks. Occasionally she is able to look up, her face swollen and blotched ruddy.

I continue to pray for her, and to listen to God. After a half hour of singing, the discipline of worship is doing its work in my heart, softening it, filling me. I try to forgive Scot, ask for God's help in our marriage, our life. During one song where we are seated, singing, I'm moved to stand and lift my arms. My eyes shut, I sing, pray, plead with God to intervene in my own private troubles.

Suddenly I feel an arm around me and the woman from the end of the aisle is crying on my shoulder, sobbing. I sing over her "nothing is impossible with God" and hold her. I am amazed at this—but I go with it, because I think I have just stumbled into a God space. I end up standing in front of my husband, who is seated, and likely dumbfounded.

He moves over so that I can stand next to the woman. As the worship continues around us, I pray out loud, into the woman's ear that she would be healed of whatever pain she's going through. Soon, out pours a story of a jerk of a boyfriend who kicked her out of his car 25 miles from home. She's intent on telling me her story, even as the music wafts around us.

I tell her she does not deserve to be treated like that, and that God has better things for her. I try to keep my answers brief, quiet, try to limit the conversation, which I'm sure is disturbing people around us.

She tells me she texted him but he did not respond. I tell her she should not be in touch with him, that he's a jerk. I tell her she must delete his name and number from her phone, and she obediently digs in her purse to get the phone out. Together we delete several messages and his number. The worship around us continues.

After the service, we talk more. The man with her is her group leader from our Divorce Recovery ministry, who tells me I am "a Godsend."

Maybe worship equips us to be sent, to whoever needs to hear truth, to feel an undemanding human touch that communicates truth: God loves you. God has better things for you.

## Noticing and Naming

Just as worship is not restricted to music, neither is it limited to service. Worship is honoring God. It is loving God. Worship invites us to notice and name the work of God in the world. Using our gifts can easily become about us and our skills. That's why we're invited to offer a living sacrifice that is directed toward God, not ourselves.

The ancient poetry of the Bible has this wonderful word that describes this noticing and naming. "Ascribe to the LORD." *Ascribe* means "to attribute to," "to give credit to."

When we ascribe something to the Lord, we are giving credit where credit is due. We're saying—it's not us, it's God.

> **Ascribe** to the LORD the glory due his name; bring an offering and come before him. **Worship** the LORD in the splendor of his holiness. (1 Chron. 16:29, emphases added)
>
> Ascribe to the LORD the glory due his name; worship the LORD in the splendor of his holiness. (Ps. 29:2)

It's one thing to say that we give God glory, that we give credit where credit is due. But what does it look like to live this way?

As we discussed earlier, we worship when we notice and name evidence of God wherever we encounter beauty, truth, or presence. God invites us to do just that.

The daily prayer of Jews for centuries: Hear O Israel, the Lord our God, the Lord is one. Called the Shema, or Sh'ma, in Hebrew it is *Sh'ma Yisra'eil Adonai Eloheinu Adonai echad.*

Traditionally, it is also the prayer devout people say upon arising, and just before going to sleep. The Sh'ma bookends the day, creating a frame around it. Within that frame, we can notice the work of God in the world.

A look at the context of this prayer in Scripture invites us to make our daily round a God space. To notice and name the work of God as we go through our day.

> Hear, O Israel: The LORD our God, the LORD is one. Love the LORD your God with all your heart and with all your soul and with all your strength. These commandments

that I give you today are to be on your hearts. Impress them on your children. Talk about them when you sit at home and when you walk along the road, when you lie down and when you get up. Tie them as symbols on your hands and bind them on your foreheads. Write them on the doorframes of your houses and on your gates. (Deut. 6:4–9)

Deuteronomy 11:19 reiterates, "Teach them [God's truths] to your children, talking about them when you sit at home and when you walk along the road, when you lie down and when you get up."

When we walk to the park, drive in the minivan, sit at home, or stroll through our office on the way to a meeting, how can we notice and point out the beauty of creation, the truth in a story, or the strength of God's presence, whether in difficulty or joy? How can we proclaim the glory of God in our everyday "walking along the road"?

A Psalm I memorized as a child proclaims, "I will bless the Lord at all times: his praise shall continually be in my mouth" (Ps. 34:1, KJV).

Another says, "Bless the Lord, O my soul: and all that is within me, bless his holy name" (Ps. 103:1, KJV).

When we worship, we stop demanding blessings from God and turn it around to bless God. We praise God—which is not the same as saying thank you for blessings. It's more like we say to God, *Thank you for being you. You're worthy of admiration, of praise, just because of who you are.* Worship is about responding to the extravagant, crazy love God gives us with crazy, extravagant love right back. Worship transforms us.

Our transformation—our changes in attitudes and actions—is itself worship.

Making God our top priority shifts the focus of our lives away from ourselves, asks us to serve others as if we were serving Jesus. It can be inconvenient. Worship holds a tension: We bring our sacrifice, be it service, singing, or focus, and turn it away from ourselves and toward God. We bless God and are blessed by doing so. Worship is both a spiritual practice and a response to God. That response offers us a path to intimacy and presence.

Worship can become rote and even stale if we are not attuned to new and different ways God invites us to connect. What kind of worship space is God inviting you into? In what new or different ways might you notice and name God's work to be drawn into deeper intimacy with the Almighty?

When we notice and name the work of God in the world, we realign our souls. We reorder our priorities, preparing our hearts to seek God. This realignment stirs in us a desire for simplicity, for singular focus on God. It is to that practice we will turn next.

# Simplicity

## *Space in My Soul*

My house is cluttered. As much as I might aspire to it, I'm not a minimalist. I'm a minimalist wannabe. Surely that counts for something, right?

I'm not into status or having the best stuff—it's just sometimes hard for me to clear out the mediocre stuff that clogs up my kitchen and my office. I'm not a big shopper—frankly, it bores me. But I tend to hang on to things for far too long, you know, just in case. Those things tend to pile up.

I often try to blame this on my husband, who lives in a whirlwind of paper and clutter much of the time. But I'm not much better. At best, I have little islands of organization in the messy sea that is my real, imperfect life. "Organized" is not a way anyone describes me. It's sometimes hard for me to let go of things: books, clothes, papers, photos, kitchen gadgets, files. I run my business from my home, which is my favorite excuse for the paperwork clogging cabinets and a closet.

I sit down to write a chapter on simplicity and think, *Maybe I should clean out that closet first to earn some quick credibility.* I confuse organizing and simplifying with simplicity.

Simplicity is not the same as organizing. Ironically, *Real Simple* magazine rarely includes articles about simplicity as a spiritual practice. Instead, it offers tips on organizing your stuff, and also, countless ads for *more stuff to buy*.

The Christian practice of simplicity is not about space in my closet; it's about space in my soul. I long for simplicity, but I'm sometimes unsure what that even means. Less stuff, less worry, less distraction, a sharper focus on what really matters. I want a clear path to God, to walk unhindered with Jesus, and maybe the clutter, both within me and around me, is getting in my way.

Simplifying and organizing are helpful tasks, but they will not deepen my intimacy with God. If that's what I truly long for, I need to unclutter my soul first. I need to realign my soul with God.

Richard Foster writes, "The Christian Discipline of simplicity is an *inward* reality that results in an *outward* lifestyle."[1] Foster warns that trying to only outwardly simplify will lead to legalism, and will never satisfy the craving of our souls.

That inward reality—soul realignment—is where the adventure begins, and if it is authentic, it leads to a visible change in lifestyle. We don't need as much stuff. We're able to be more generous because we are less attached to our stuff. We don't need to fill an inner ache by accruing. Our embodied spirituality will match our inner attitudes and affections.

## Soul Realignment

What really matters? What happens inside your tired, hurried heart when you hear that question? For me, it stirs a longing.

The truth is, realignment sometimes hurts. It means loss, or at least letting go. When we ask, "What really matters?" we might have to face the truth that we're hanging on to things that *don't* matter. What might have been helpful in the past just weighs us down now.

Simplicity as a practice offers us freedom. According to Jesus, it's connected less to our stuff and more to our mental and emotional clutter. The biggest barrier to true simplicity is not a messy desk or an overcrowded closet. According to Jesus, what keeps us from simplicity is the sin of worry.

Jesus said, "Therefore I tell you, do not worry about your life, what you will eat or drink; or about your body, what you will wear. Is not life more than food, and the body more than clothes?" (Matt. 6:25).

Do. Not. Worry. Similar in form and content to Jesus's other favorite directive, "Do not be afraid." Worrying about stuff keeps us from living in simplicity.

Why do we cling to our stuff? Why do we accumulate and then feel overwhelmed? It's worry that we won't have enough, that God will not provide food and clothing and also, peace down deep in the place where worry wrings its tired hands.

Jesus's words are more than a suggestion. How do we follow his instruction and not worry? I need a strategy for that.

Jesus offers a very specific practice to combat worry, to realign our souls. He invites us to notice. Consider the birds, he says. Back away from the screen, get outside, and actually look at birds—and while you're at it, flowers. This is not fluffy, vapid, Hallmark card–y advice. Too much of our life is lived indoors, focused on worry and stress and political Facebook posts and bad news about terror and war. The first step toward simplicity, Jesus says, is to close the laptop, stand up, and walk outside. Open your eyes, look up into the sky and trees, and just let that sink in. Meditate on the birds. Watch them gather seeds, bits of grass, insects they pull out of the dirt like magic. Watch them soar. We are invited to live our lives, not apart from our bodies in the world, but in them. See birds. Breathe air. Feel the grass and dirt beneath our feet. The world, which Jesus made, is still here and in it are birds and flowers and sky that Jesus designed with us in mind—beauty that would realign our souls if we'd only pay attention, notice, be attentive. Which sounds a lot like worship, doesn't it?

> Look at the birds of the air; they do not sow or reap or store away in barns, and yet your heavenly Father feeds them. Are you not much more valuable than they? Can any one of you by worrying add a single hour to your life?
>
> And why do you worry about clothes? See how the flowers of the field grow. They do not labor or spin. Yet I tell you that not even Solomon in all his splendor was dressed like one of these. If that is how God clothes the grass of the field, which is here today and tomorrow is thrown into the fire, will he not much more clothe you—you of little faith? So do not worry, saying, "What shall we eat?" or "What shall we drink?" or "What shall we wear?" For the pagans run after all these things, and your heavenly Father knows that you need them. (Matt. 6:26–32)

Your heavenly Father knows. God knows what you need, not just clothes and food and drink but also intimate, soul-satisfying love.

Jesus continues, offering a strategy to realign our souls, to embrace the practice of simplicity:

But seek first his kingdom and his righteousness, and all these things will be given to you as well. Therefore do not worry about tomorrow, for tomorrow will worry about itself. Each day has enough trouble of its own. (Matt. 6:33–34)

Jesus taught more about the kingdom of God than any other topic, but he used parables and metaphor to describe it: the kingdom was like a pearl of great price, or yeast in bread, or an overseer who pays the workers hired late in the day the same as those who've been there since sunrise, or a father who forgives a prodigal son.

In contrast to his contemporaries' expectations of a political or physical kingdom, Jesus talked about a spiritual reality.

One day the Pharisees asked Jesus, "When will the Kingdom of God come?"

Jesus replied, "The Kingdom of God can't be detected by visible signs. You won't be able to say, 'Here it is!' or 'It's over there!' For the Kingdom of God is already among you." (Luke 17:20–21 NLT)

To seek the kingdom of God means we step down from the throne of our lives, echoing Jesus's prayer to God the Father, "not my will but yours be done." When we "seek first" God's kingdom, we make God's priorities our own, allow our lives to be God infused, God focused. We put others before ourselves and filter our decisions through a simple grid: Will this action, this choice, express love to God and to my neighbor?

When a new king or president takes over a nation, power realigns, the laws sometimes change, priorities shift. In the same way, God's kingdom, ushered into our life, causes realignment within our souls. Often, that shift changes our actions—we become people who live out kingdom values like hospitality, worship, generosity, simplicity, and gratitude.

Whole books have been written about the kingdom of God. In this context, Jesus invites us to trade worry for a divine perspective, in which we realize we are safe, loved, free—and in that freedom, we can trust. We can, as the Psalm says, cease striving and know that God is God. (See Psalm 46.) It is then that our lives become simple—because we put first things first.

So much of our life is tangled in dissatisfaction, feeling like we need just a little more. A little more stuff, a little bigger house, that new outfit, a little more love, a promotion, a little better marriage. Jesus says to first seek God, then all these things will take their proper place in your life—as add-ons, not the main thing.

## Simplicity versus Duplicity

The opposite of simplicity is not complexity but duplicity. Simplicity is focused on seeking first the kingdom of God. Duplicity is trying to seek God while also trying to seek first another thing—wealth, security, approval, or even love of other people. But two things cannot be first. What the Bible calls double mindedness will always hinder us. Seek first the kingdom, Jesus said, and all these things will be "added to you." God will take care of them, if you let them go.

What do you chase after, what do you want more of? That question is not intended to shame us but to free us. Stop chasing what cannot satisfy. Seek God first. The kingdom is not some faraway reality, Jesus said. It's right now, right here, among you—if only you can look and see it. Seek it, and you'll find.

As we realign our souls, the inner reality can and should impact our outer reality, as Foster says. When we embrace the inconvenient adventure of letting go, of simplicity, we find an unexpected benefit: freedom.

Then begins a beautiful dance: We focus first on God, seeking the kingdom. Our stuff takes a less important role; our outward reality begins to change. We don't need to be that busy, to have that much stuff. We let go, and when we do, experience even more freedom.

I can beat myself up over my less than perfect house, or I can instead celebrate the inward reality of simplicity that has been growing slowly over time. Slowly that inner reality has begun to change my closet, my calendar, and my commitments.

## Letting Go to Take Hold of Joy

My closet has plenty of clothes that I've owned for years. Some, like my favorite jeans, I wear often. Others gather dust. They still fit even if they're not in style or don't suit my taste.

In her best-selling book *The Life-Changing Magic of Tidying Up*, Marie Kondo instructs readers in "the Japanese art of decluttering and organizing." Under this method, you can massively reduce your inventory of clothing, papers, and junk by physically handling each item and asking, "Does this item spark joy?" If not, you don't keep it. If it sparked joy when you bought it but it no longer does, don't keep it. Donate it or throw it away, creating space in your closet, and ultimately your life.

"I chose this standard for a reason," Kondo writes. "After all, what is the point in tidying? If it's not so that our space and the things in it can bring us happiness, then I think there is no point at all.... Keep only those things that speak to your heart. Then take the plunge and discard all the rest. By doing this, you can reset your life and embark on a new lifestyle."[2]

I'm not espousing everything in Kondo's book, but I love her self-awareness. She points out that our stuff represents a lot of our inner reality. The practice of simplicity goes far beyond simplifying, or organizing, but it may look like that externally. Simplicity is an inner reality that impacts our outer reality. When we're content at a soul level, we can also be content on a material level.

So on a recent Saturday, I paw through my closet, take hold of each item, and ask, "Does this spark joy?" It's an odd question, difficult to answer. Kondo says if it used to spark joy but no longer does, discard it. Some items, I know right away—nope. Doesn't fit right, color makes me look washed out, it's twenty years old, and I never wear it anyway. As Kondo suggests, I say, "Thank you" to each item. Weird, right? But it does somehow make it easier to toss them. Pretty soon, the clothes left in the closet are apparently feeling appreciated and I have a huge pile of clothes I've bid a grateful farewell to, that I will take to Goodwill.

A number of the items in my closet were given to me by a friend. She shopped a lot and ended up with things she didn't really want, and when she'd clean out her closet, she would offer them to me. Some items still had the tags on them. At the time, it felt generous and kind, because my clothing budget was basically zero. Some I loved, others weren't exactly my style. I didn't have a defined style, unless you count old Levi's and sweatshirts as a style. Her gifts looked nice, and most of them fit me, but many simply weren't me. But I didn't know that at the time, because my soul was cluttered, preventing me from knowing myself.

For reasons I don't fully understand, that friend has moved on, severing ties with me without explaining why. At first, I wanted to try to hang on to the friendship, to demand an explanation for the drift, to cling. But I hadn't done that. I'd let it fade away, because I didn't know if the relationship was worth fighting for. It's dysfunctional to pursue someone who has dumped you. But sorting through clothes and realizing many of them were her hand-me-downs, I realized I had not completely let go. I felt sad all over again. I wondered if I had put this friendship on a back shelf of my heart. As I asked, "Does this blouse spark joy? Do these pants spark joy?" it occurred to me also to ask, "Does this friendship spark joy?" My answer was "It sparks sadness and confusion and hurt."

Part of the healing was to place on the Goodwill pile many of the clothes she discarded by giving to me. My heart got lighter with each item I tossed on the pile. I was letting go, moving on, forgiving and releasing. I "thanked" each blouse and pair of pants for serving me well and I also said thank you to this friend. *Thank you for blessing my life, for a season of friendship.* I visualized saying thank you and letting her go. The exercise made me aware of how much I'd been hanging on to the pain of loss, how I needed to simply say thank you and release her, and my feelings about our ended friendship, so I could move forward and find peace.

What we hang on to tells us a story about ourselves, sometimes a painful one. The relationships we hang on to also tell a story. Letting go may hurt more than ignoring them, but removing them will set us free. Releasing the person, and any bitterness that's built up like dust on the shoulders of a jacket hung in the back of a closet, brings a lightness, a God space in the closet of the soul.

## My Calendar

Often, what keeps me from living a life of simplicity is my inability to say no, especially when it comes to being busy. I take on too much, often because I am addicted to my own sense of competence and accomplishment. They provide me with heavy doses of self-worth.

Our calendar and all the obligations in it reflect the turmoil in our souls, the longing to be included, the fear of letting people down, the fear of missing opportunities.

Being busy makes us feel significant. It's why we overschedule ourselves. We all need self-esteem and to feel loved and capable—that's okay. But we seek that significance in the wrong place, and it never satisfies the way intimacy with God does. Deep friendship with God, knowing that God is with us, that he loves and accepts us, provides a surer and longer lasting sense of significance than all the accomplishments and busyness in the world.

Work can take up a big chunk of our calendar, and some of that can't be helped. But sometimes we have to make changes in order to save our souls, to seek first God's kingdom.

I've been writing books, and doing what I call authoring, for about twenty years. Authoring is more than writing. It's the unglamorous parts, the mundane and essential. It is writing books on behalf of other people, hours spent building a platform, marketing your work, taking freelance assignments to get your name out there, managing and juggling deadlines, invoicing, administration, and speaking. Speaking at retreats, events, conferences, church luncheons crowded with eager women looking to be inspired between the chicken salad and dessert. For years, I stood up and talked at any number of these events, as part of my authoring work. (I sometimes still do.) I didn't have an assistant, so I did my own scheduling. Booked my own flights, sent my own invoices, created handouts, and ran my own book table. Sometimes, without intending to, I ended up speaking seven times in two weeks. It got to the point one year where I couldn't talk about my fall schedule without getting a little teary. On top of the speaking I was cranking out books, articles, blog posts. And I was a mom and wife and church volunteer. But what drained me most was the speaking and the travel it required.

When you're an author, you feel pressure to get out and tell your story, share your wisdom, hopefully sell some books. You get to meet your readers, shake their hands, look into their eyes and realize with a start that what you wrote connected with their hearts. It reminds you that the hard work and low pay is worth it. You find out people didn't just buy your book, they actually read it, and it somehow made a difference.

Going to churches and talking about Jesus and spiritual stuff could easily be classified under "seeking first God's kingdom." It's an essential part of authoring. In certain seasons of my life, I've felt clearly called to teach, to speak. In other seasons, writing and parenting took top priority. To seek first God's kingdom I had to listen, and be willing to flex and respond when the divine assignment shifted. I was seeking God's kingdom, but I needed to listen to *how* God wanted me to do that. Seeking first God's kingdom means first paying attention. Seeking first the kingdom means seeking to learn what your role in that kingdom should be—and what it should not be.

Most authors will tell you that writing and speaking are two different skills. Some writers speak because they have to. Others are speakers who write but would prefer to just stand up in front of people and talk.

I taught classes, led retreats, and spoke at events, and people affirmed that I did it well. I enjoyed it occasionally, but I didn't love it. And I didn't love the travel that took me away from my family. Yet, for many years, my fall speaking schedule took me out of town about half the weekends between Labor Day and Thanksgiving, and I worked full-time during the week. My calendar in those years was crowded with carpools and kids' sports, speaking and writing deadlines, time with friends and family, and church volunteer work—which also involved speaking. When I overcommitted to out-of-town speaking gigs, I missed soccer games and ordinary moments hanging out with my family. Any working parent who also has to travel for work will tell you that it's hard enough to juggle family and work commitments, and traveling adds another layer of complexity to the mix.

Speaking puts you in front of a lot of people. But you are alone. You walk through airports alone. You're in your hotel alone. It's lonely. It's you alone behind that podium, looking out at people who have a variety of expectations (Entertain me! Teach me! Make me laugh! Make me cry! Give me some spiritually deep stuff! Don't challenge me too much!), all of which you cannot possibly meet because they contradict one another.

Too often, women's retreats or events mean more scrutiny on what a speaker wears than what she says. "Great talk, but um—when we said you could be casual we didn't think you'd wear jeans." Or, "My friends and I really loved listening to you—and we especially love those boots! Where did you get them?" (That is actual feedback from both event organizers and participants at the same event, which inspired me to hang up my speaker boots for a while.)

I got to the point where I was burned out on speaking. It drained me, and I felt pressured. Eventually, speaking wore me out both emotionally and physically. Stress and work and kids and a really difficult season in my marriage took a toll, even impacting my physical health. I needed desperately to slow down.

It took me a while, but I ruthlessly cut back my speaking schedule. It wasn't just the pressure or the weird critiques that people gave me. It wasn't just the fact that my pulse was racing even when I was sitting still. It was also a decision born of a deep desire to pay attention to God, to not miss my life while I ran through it.

I saw the time with my kids sluicing past like water running downhill, and I didn't want to miss my last few years with my kids before they went off to college. I had the rest of my life to speak, but the four years in front of me were the one and only time I'd get to be at home with my teens. In times of prayer, God kept bringing to mind the idea that this was the fourth and final quarter of the game, and often that is when games are won or lost. I needed to focus my efforts at home, to finish well, to finish strong.

I kept writing—I didn't have the luxury to not work, but I could do work that didn't put me on the road. I also said no to any requests that I write without pay, or for miniscule pay—something writers get asked to do all the time. That enabled me to work, but for my work hours to be efficient and productive. I took on more collaborative projects (sometimes called ghostwriting or coauthoring), which paid better and kept me behind the scenes, which was what I needed. I deliberately took time to care for myself. I took control of my calendar. I took assignments that were worth my time. I ended up writing or cowriting four books in one year. But I was mostly home, writing while my kids were at school. I finally had the right kind of soul realignment.

That decision led to growth in my career and, more important, connection with my family. While my children were in high school, I traveled very little. I spoke at local churches, did occasional one-day events rather than speaking at weekend retreats. That opened space for new opportunities, new writing projects, new skills learned. Looking back, now that my kids are thriving in their twenties, I am so thankful.

We all have opportunities—but that doesn't mean we should always say yes. Sometimes, the first step toward simplicity is saying no, even to things that seem good or helpful.

Simplicity calls us to live with a singular focus, to make the main thing the main thing. And in that season, it needed to be my children, my health, and my writing. In order to say yes to those things, I had to say no to a crazy travel schedule. I have no regrets. In fact, my life seemed infused with more joy, more contentment. I felt more connected to my family and to God. We simplify, narrow our focus, to what matters—even if only for a season.

I'm in a new season now; my kids are out of the house. I can travel if I choose. I'm trying to pay attention, to figure out if that's something I should say yes to.

I've slowly added some speaking gigs for the coming year, choosing carefully what I say yes to and what I say no to. But I also have the freedom to listen to God's direction and other assignments. I still love collaborative writing and running my writing business.

I think for many of us, our calendars are the hardest to bring into alignment with our values of simplicity. As parents, our calendars are crowded with not just our own obligations but our children's: sports and school, playdates and pediatrician appointments, music shows and miscellany.

What obligations have you put on your calendar? What have you said yes to that you regret? Did you say yes to God, or yes to making other people happy? Have you said yes to things that don't really fit with keeping a singular focus? How are your yeses affecting your relationships? Your physical and emotional health?

Do you find yourself saying, "I'm so busy!"? Busy doing what? Whatever makes us feel busy, hurried, or frazzled are things we perhaps shouldn't have said yes to in the first place. I can spend eight hours a day writing, and I don't feel busy doing it. I feel joyful and productive and challenged, because it's both hard and fun. I learn as I write, which always turns my crank, because I feel God's smile when I write.

Often, we're busy with the activities of other people: our kids, spouse, or aging parents. We can't opt out of caring for others, but we can model a sane pace of life for our families. I learned the hard way—letting my calendar reach a point past my control and hitting the wall with my health and sanity— that limits were healthy. The things I felt exhausted doing for God, the Lord had never asked me to do.

Choose simplicity when it comes to your calendar. Simplify by deciding ahead of time what limits you'll place on your activities and commitments, and those of your children. Ask God to guide you as you decide what to say yes to and what to say no to.

## My Commitments

Commitments end up on our calendar, so these two areas are related. But commitments go beyond activities and appointments. These are longer-term obligations that are not a one-and-done but last for a season: volunteering for a church ministry or a nonprofit organization or the PTA, taking a class or joining a small group, playing in a sports league or on a team, even relationships and friendships.

Most of us also have financial commitments: a mortgage or rent, maybe a car payment or other debt. Many of us are overcommitted financially, and our practice of simplicity is sabotaged by those commitments.

Commitments often disguise themselves as "Oh, it's just one meeting a month" or "It's ten easy payments of $29.99." But if we sign up for four separate "just once a month" commitments, we're suddenly stuck with a weekly obligation on our calendar. Those ten $29.99 payments, in reality, equal $300.

Overcommitment keeps us from simplicity. Choosing our commitments carefully brings us freedom, which is what we long for, and ultimately what simplicity promises us.

I drive a fifteen-year-old Ford Escape, which has a large tumor of rust growing on the right rear fender. It sometimes leaks a little oil, has more than a few door dings. But it's paid for, and it does well in our snowy Chicago winters. I said no to the commitment of a car payment. By saying no to that commitment, I was able to say yes to the commitment of helping my kids pay for college, and my commitment to give generously to my church or a ministry. This is where simplicity is not so Pinterest worthy, where freedom looks like a rusty Ford.

Commitments are not all bad, of course. In some seasons, it's wonderful to volunteer at your child's school. It's essential to commit to caring for an aging parent. But when we wonder why simplicity seems elusive, we have to take our commitments into account. What have you committed to?

## Relational Capacity

Another factor in practicing simplicity is our relational world. It's easy in our culture to have a lot of acquaintances (or Facebook friends) but still feel lonely or isolated because we don't really go deep with anyone. Managing large networks of people we don't know very well is not only stressful, it can keep us from the freedom of simplicity.

I'm what I call a friendly introvert. I love people, I am blessed with friendships, but I am energized by time alone. I enjoy practicing hospitality, and I love a crowd around my table. I also love solitude, to balance that out. I need both in my life.

I've lived in the same general area for most of my life, and in the same neighborhood for more than twenty years, and I've attended the same church for almost thirty years. Because of this, I have several circles of friends whom I've treasured for more than a quarter century. I also have relationships with people I've met in recent years or even months, whom I'm still getting to know. I value both new and long-term relationships.

Each friendship is a commitment, a promise to connect and engage on a variety of levels. We often misjudge our relational capacity. We think more is better, but quantity will eventually erode quality. We can't be best friends with everyone. We each may have a different relational capacity, but none of us has unlimited capacity, for friendships or anything else. When we spread ourselves too thin, we may eventually find ourselves with a bunch of acquaintances and an aching loneliness.

One tribe I'm a part of is the neighborhood moms, all of

whom have kids about the same age as mine. Many of them are people I met volunteering in our kids' kindergarten classes or serving on the PTA. We used to drive in carpools together; now our kids are in college and we would rarely see each other if we didn't make the effort. So we make the effort. Once a month, about fifteen of us get together to celebrate whoever's birthday falls in that month. We all bring appetizers and desserts and wine, and just catch up. We take turns hosting, or sometimes go out. I'm committed to connecting with these women.

I'm blessed with these long-term friendships. But friendships are not always easy, and they don't always last forever. Sometimes they last for a season, and then they fade.

I have lost friends—often those I'd consider especially close. I wonder if it's me. I know I can be intense, and a little intimidating. Friendship with me can be exhausting. I've been described as "tightly wound," and I take a certain sick pride in that. My top StrengthsFinder profile is "achiever." I get stuff done, sister. I overcompensate, overfunction (that's my therapist's word, not mine). My solution to fix whatever's broken is to work harder. This has caused some relational casualties along the way.

I grieve the loss of a best friend from my children's preschool years who moved away and lost touch. I'm saddened by the disconnection from the friend whose hand-me-downs I discarded, and with them, my expectations of reconnection. Another friend, mired in depression over a great disappointment in her own life, seems unresponsive to my efforts to connect. The distance suddenly between us makes me feel helpless.

Sometimes, friendships are worth fighting for. But other times, we have to let them go, accept the fact that people move away, whether to a new location or a new social circle, and they leave us behind. No matter how hard we work, we can't always fix it. When we're living in the simplicity that seeks God first, we are free to let go of relationships that need to be released.

When we realize we have all acquaintances and no deep friendships, we have to focus and edit and be intentional about how we invest our time. Commitments—friendship, marriage—are reciprocal. If they are not, they slide into co-dependency. Choose to simplify by pruning them from your life, or making them healthier by changing your own behavior. Pruning leads to growth, and that's true with friendships as well. To lose a friend is a severe mercy that creates space we didn't know we needed, for growth we never dreamed possible.

## Generosity and Simplicity

Jesus said,

For where your treasure is, there your heart will be also.

The eye is the lamp of the body. If your eyes are healthy, your whole body will be full of light. But if your eyes are unhealthy, your whole body will be full of darkness. If then the light within you is darkness, how great is that darkness!

No one can serve two masters. Either you will hate the one and love the other, or you will be devoted to the one and despise the other. You cannot serve both God and money. (Matt. 6:21–24)

Simplicity is, in part, about our stuff, and the thing we trade for stuff: money. Money and the kingdom of God were two of Jesus's favorite discussion topics.

This odd passage in his teaching on money and treasure talks about our eyes. What does it mean to have "healthy eyes"? Older versions of the Bible render Jesus's statement this way: "The light of the body is the eye: if therefore thine eye be single, thy whole body shall be full of light" (Matt. 6:22 KJV). A "single eye"? What is that? This phrase is one that gets lost in translation, and we miss out on something profound.

The "single eye" is a translation of an ancient idea that has no direct English translation. Richard Foster wrote about it this way: "It refers both to a single aim in life and to a generous, unselfish spirit. The two ideas have such a close connection in the Hebrew mind that they can be expressed in a single phrase. Singleness of purpose toward God and generosity of spirit are twins."[3]

When we seek first the kingdom of God, when we have that singular focus, that single purpose of following God, we let go of our tight-fisted grasp on our stuff, our resources. We're suddenly free from fear, and therefore free to be generous.

In the letter I mentioned earlier, my daughter, Melanie, thanked me for instilling the value of "simple living," but she lives much more simply than I do. She drives a twenty-year-old Toyota, although she often takes the bus. She is incredibly thrifty. One year during college she decided not to buy any new clothes, as an exercise in simplicity and also because, as she said, "I had too many clothes and didn't want to acquire more as I moved around a lot during college."

When I asked her what she learned from that year of choosing not to shop for clothes, she said it wasn't really anything deep, but just that she didn't need so many clothes. However, when I asked her to make recommendations about how to live simply, off the top of her head she texted back to me:

Buy less stuff, travel more, don't have a big house, don't eat out a ton, don't put worth in what you own (drive a 20 yr. old Camry!) but be generous to others…?

Generosity and simplicity are intricately linked. When we live simply, we use less of our resources for ourselves, and we have more available to give to others, or to invest in what God is doing in the world.

What does a generosity grounded in simplicity look like? That's what we'll explore in the next chapter.

# Generosity

## *Space in My Budget*

I have been married twenty-five years. In a row. To the same person. This has required more prayer, sweat, and tears than you can imagine. It's not been easy, but I think most couples, if honest, would never say marriage is easy. A lot of people who knew us when we got married would not have put money on our odds of making it this far. But for better or worse, here we are.

Marriage has required both of us to be generous—to give more than we thought we were getting. A fifty-fifty marriage is doomed. We must both feel as if we are giving 100 percent. I have not always lived up to this ideal, I can readily admit.

God calls us to be generous not for generosity's sake, but for the sake of relationship. Whether we are generous with time, money, forgiveness, or grace, we do so in the context of relationship. It is how God loves us—lavishly—and calls us to love others.

The practice of generosity is not just financial, but relational. We're called to be generous with our funds as well as with our emotional energy. I love the language of Isaiah 58:10, which invites us to "spend yourselves in behalf of the hungry and satisfy the needs of the oppressed." To "spend yourself" sounds like full engagement, a greater commitment than an online donation click.

Whether in a marriage, a friendship, a church community, or a relationship with an extended family, or with our kids, God calls us to give extravagantly—to give up our life in order to gain it, to give rather than receive and find the blessing buried in it, to invite God into the space of our relationships. Jesus said in order to gain your life, you've got to lose it, and that to love means to lay down your life, and your agenda, for others.

My parents live in California, as does most of my extended family. My dad has one brother and one sister, they each have a spouse and one child. That's it. My only brother lives in Arizona. We talk and text, but I see him only every few years. My mother's family has all passed away, and so my extended family is very small.

My husband, on the other hand, was one of five children, and for many years, all of his siblings lived near us. They are forever up in each other's business, squabbling but also taking care of one another in ways that were unfamiliar to me. Scot's parents are snowbirds, spending summers in Wisconsin and winters in Florida. His sister lives in the same town we do and works part-time for my husband. His older brother (and his wife and two daughters) lives in Milwaukee. We see all of them a lot.

My kids grew up with regular interactions with their cousins and aunts and uncles, something I didn't have growing up. My in-laws' home in Wisconsin, about a ninety-minute drive from our house, is on a lake. Especially when my kids were small, we spent many summer weekends at the lake, which is not as idyllic as it sounds. It was chaotic and loud, and we often got recruited for home repair or maintenance projects, but my kids still loved it. The best part was that my mother-in-law would babysit for my kids while Scot and I went sailing.

In 2002, my husband's younger brother, Tom, died unexpectedly of a heart attack, at age thirty-four. The tragedy wounded the whole family so deeply, especially my mother-in-law. Her loss, even today, is palpable.

Prior to Tom's death, we would get together with Scot's siblings for holidays, if we happened to be in town. Tom, the bachelor uncle, used to come over early Easter morning to our house, sneak into the backyard, and hide candy-filled plastic eggs for my kids and my niece to find. He'd bring the mashed potatoes at Thanksgiving.

After he died, the holiday gatherings came to an abrupt halt. He died in September, and that Thanksgiving no one wanted to gather. No one talked about it. It just stopped. For a few years, I took my husband and kids out to California to visit my family for Thanksgiving. We started celebrating Easter with other family friends. My parents came to our house for Christmas. I was curious and grieved about the fact that Scot's family seemed to no longer even want to celebrate holidays. It's hard to gather when someone is so profoundly missing, when their absence creates a gaping wound at the table.

But one year, we simply couldn't fit a trip to California into the budget, financially or timewise, at Thanksgiving. And I said to Scot, "Let's have your family over. It's time."

I love my husband's family. But we could not be more different. They vote differently than I do. My father-in-law listens to Rush Limbaugh daily, and Fox News is on 24/7 at their home. They don't share our faith tradition. They tend, like big families sometimes do, to be kind of loud and enthusiastic and a little bossy. For about the first decade of my marriage, I felt a little like an outsider in the family. They were polite, even kind. But there was a distance, probably created by me as much as them. They were just really different from my family, from what felt normal to me.

But after several years of pain and unspoken grief, God nudged me. I realized that none of them had the strength, even several years after Tom's death, to host and plan a holiday gathering, to be the one who unjammed the logs of grief. And God honestly sat me down and said, *I have put you in a family, now love them. They're not just Scot's family, they're yours as well.*

I objected that they probably didn't want to come, that I was an outsider and not the one who should pull the family together. Why did I need to be generous to them? I got along with them just fine, but I didn't feel that close. Of course they were not my enemies, but I didn't think of them as dear friends, either. But God asked me to be generous, to be an agent of healing, to become a kinder friend to them. To initiate friendship and healing.

Jesus called us to radical generosity, asking us to love extravagantly, lend indiscriminately, be kind and merciful without reservation. In other words, to imitate him:

If you love those who love you, what credit is that to you? Even sinners love those who love them. And if you do good to those who are good to you, what credit is that to you? Even sinners do that. And if you lend to those from whom you expect repayment, what credit is that to you? Even sinners lend to sinners, expecting to be repaid in full. But love your enemies, do good to them, and lend to them without expecting to get anything back. Then your reward will be great, and you will be children of the Most High, because he is kind to the ungrateful and wicked. Be merciful, just as your Father is merciful. (Luke 6:32–36)

Again, my husband's family members were not my "enemies" but simply people I was not close to. We got along pretty well, and I saw them a lot, spent quite a bit of time with them, especially at the lake in the summer. But I felt like they were his people, not mine.

But God asked me to embrace the inconvenience of generosity, to welcome those who seemed distant. So the best way I know how to love people, is to feed them. To gather them, feed them, invite them to talk to one another. So, I decided to host Thanksgiving.

His parents were already in Florida that year, and Scot's younger sister, Judy, had moved to Texas. But we invited his older brother and sister, and their families, to come to our house.

I told Scot about my plan to not just feed them but to have everyone share what they felt thankful for. "My family doesn't do that," he said. "They aren't into talking about feelings and stuff like that."

I knew that was true, but I didn't care. They were free to pass on sharing if they wanted. If I was the one hosting, I could set the parameters. They were grown-ups; they could handle it. And they did. And now they love meals at our home.

These days, I host Thanksgiving and Easter regularly, gathering both friends and Scot's family around our table. And I count Scot's siblings and their partners and children as my own family. Our relationship is no longer superficial. By choosing to be generous, I moved from indifference to love. By choosing to be generous, I expanded my tribe. Coincidentally, I destroyed my own insecurities.

We're still very different. But the inconvenient practice of generosity has transformed our relationships. It has added texture, nuance, and a little noise to my life. They haven't replaced my own family but simply expanded it.

It's not always easy. And God always makes more space for generosity, challenges me to continue to love extravagantly.

Two weeks before the manuscript for this book was due to my editor, I was faithfully working away, writing six days a week while juggling a couple of other clients. I felt good about my progress, how the project was coming together. But there was not a lot of margin for unexpected tasks.

At that time, my mother-in-law went in for what we hoped would be a minor surgery to repair a stent in her leg. She ended up hospitalized for two days with a variety of complications.

The day she was released from the hospital, Scot and I and his brother went up to their home in Wisconsin. His younger sister flew in from Texas, alarmed by the fact that Mom had pneumonia and other issues.

My in-laws had been eating mostly frozen dinners or canned soup because my mother-in-law could not or would not cook. Scot's older sister asked if I could bring my home-made lasagna, one of my father-in-law's favorites.

I love on this family by cooking for them. It's what I do. Which is not always easy, but I don't mind it when I am not on a book deadline. Talk about inconvenient.

I assembled my homemade lasagna, then we drove to Wisconsin that evening. The next morning, we raked leaves for hours, helped get the house ready for winter. Midday, I ran inside and put the lasagna in the oven, then went out and did more work in the yard.

I gathered the family around the table for a meal, after which my husband, his brother, and his sister had a heart-to-heart conversation about plans for my in-laws' care. It was a conversation that needed to happen, and my goal was to make it slightly easier by giving everyone some tasty food first.

Spending a day and a half caring for my family, making them food, and working to prepare the lake house for winter isn't complicated. But it takes time. And I don't know about you, but for me, being generous with my time (especially when—did I mention?—I'm on deadline!) is way more challenging than being generous with my money.

Financial generosity is a challenge, but you can write a check and there you go. Most of us have enough to cover our basic needs. Most of us, even if we feel financial pressure or worry, have enough for food, shelter, and clothing. We've gone through some very lean years. Our budget may be tight, but it's time we're short of. Time is a more precious commodity to most of us than money. While you can put your expenses on a credit card if you're short of cash, there are no credit cards to loan you some extra hours in your day.

What does it look like to practice generosity with all our

resources: our money, time, homes, stuff? What about being generous with the grace we've received, the love we experience? As Jesus said, "Freely you have received; freely give" (Matt. 10:8).

It is possible to give a lot of money but not be generous with grace. Jesus invites us into a space where we hold everything loosely, where we freely share not only physical resources but grace and love as well.

Generosity flows out of simplicity, a healthy detachment from our stuff, and a focus on God. It is rarely easy because our inner two-year-old is forever shouting, "Mine!" and grabbing, holding, hoarding.

Generosity of spirit is linked with simplicity, as we discussed in the previous chapter, and living God's purpose for our lives. If we live simply, we are able to free up resources and be generous. But generosity flows not just out of a household budget surplus, but from our hearts.

How can generosity move from our attitude to our actions? What does an embodied spirituality of generosity actually look like? What does one do to live out this practice?

It's one thing to believe in helping the poor and being generous, it's another to embrace the inconvenience of forgoing what we want in order to be able to give to others. Sometimes, generosity is making lasagna and raking leaves. It's serving.

If we're seeking first the kingdom of God and his righteousness, we will put the kingdom first in our closets and calendars, *and* with our time and treasures. What we seek or pursue, we invest in.

Where is God asking you to be generous? Where is there

an invitation to give extravagantly, of your time, your money? Where may you have a generous attitude toward people who are different from you? What would that look like in your life? What benefit might you unexpectedly discover?

## How Much Is Generous?

Of course, we have to talk about money if we're talking about generosity. Money, oddly enough, was one of Jesus's favorite topics. He said you can't serve both God and money. Jesus knew that money masquerades as a god. It promises security, power, strength. But that's a lie we can debunk by changing our thoughts and our actions about money. We can only break money's power on us by choosing to be generous.

Generosity is not determined by a number or percentage, but by trust. Like Sabbath, generosity is a discipline undergirded by a countercultural concept: "enough." I have enough time, enough stuff, enough money. Our resources, whether time or money, are sufficient. God has given us a week, and asks that we give back a day: Sabbath. When we do, God gives it back to us. We have a day of rest, of reconnection with what matters.

In the same way, God's provided us resources and invites us to give back a portion. When we give back to God, we find what we gave to God becomes a gift back to us. The practice of generosity is about creating God space in our budgets and, as a result, creating God space in our hearts. Through generosity, we affirm that God can be trusted.

What often keeps people from practicing Sabbath is fear that God is unable to provide seven days of provision from six days of labor. The same fear of scarcity that keeps us from resting blocks our generosity. If I give some of my money or time or stuff away, I won't have enough. I'm afraid God won't provide.

Sabbath reminds us that we have enough time, reinforces the truth that six days' work will result, miraculously, in seven days' worth of provision. In the same way, generosity reminds us that we have enough money. We have ten dollars, we live on nine and offer one back to God to multiply and use. Nine is enough. We can trust that God's provision is enough.

The Bible's call to generosity sounds a bit like a divine throw down:

> "Bring the whole tithe into the storehouse, that there may be food in my house. Test me in this," says the LORD Almighty, "and see if I will not throw open the floodgates of heaven and pour out so much blessing that there will not be room enough to store it. I will prevent pests from devouring your crops, and the vines in your fields will not drop their fruit before it is ripe," says the LORD Almighty. (Mal. 3:10–11)

"Test me in this." Seriously? What if we were to take that challenge literally?

It's interesting that God's blessing also includes protection from financial disaster, a promise that things will go well.

What if they don't go well? What if bad stuff happens? Sometimes it does, even to good people, even to people who are generous, good, kind people. Read the book of Job, for heaven's sake. Talk to generous Christians who still face challenges.

Generosity does not inoculate us against trouble or struggle. It helps us to see differently—provides a new perspective on our pain. We do not face challenge alone. We know God is with us, protecting us, even as we struggle. We're blessed, even if we are poor, or poor in spirit.

Jesus offers a similar promise of blessing when we give:

Give, and it will be given to you. A good measure, pressed down, shaken together and running over, will be poured into your lap. For with the measure you use, it will be measured to you. (Luke 6:38)

What could show love more than generosity? We delude ourselves if we say we love but are unwilling to demonstrate it. Generosity transforms us. When we serve or give in quiet, behind the scenes ways, we demonstrate a powerful love, and we miraculously receive that love ourselves.

Author and activist Shane Claiborne offers this challenging observation:

If you ask most people what Christians believe, they can tell you, "Christians believe that Jesus is God's Son and that Jesus rose from the dead." But if you ask the average person how Christians live, they are struck silent. We have not shown the world another way of doing life. Christians pretty much live like everybody else, they just sprinkle in a little Jesus along the way.[1]

What if we could show the world another way of doing life, not just so that others can see it, but so that we are transformed?

For example, what if we chose to live on less than we earn and gave to people in need? It would demonstrate a way to live, it would help others, and might just change our hearts. A life of generosity declares that you will do more than just "sprinkle in a little Jesus."

Giving is a spiritual discipline that changes your perspective. You realize how much you have. When you give, you glimpse the abundance of God. To hoard is to live in a mindset of scarcity that robs you of intimacy with God.

I grew up tithing, and to me it makes sense. Most pastors, who depend on their congregation's giving in order to keep the lights on, preach tithing. The New Testament church went beyond percentages and "had all things in common" sharing possessions, food, money, and even land.

Some Christians argue that we just need to be "cheerful givers" (see 2 Cor. 9:7) since we're not under the law any longer. They say percentages don't matter. They do matter. If the percentage given is too small, I miss an opportunity to trust God. If I only give when I have extra, I am giving God my leftovers.

Generosity goes beyond dropping a check in the offering plate or clicking on your church's website to give online. Generosity notices needs, and partners with God to meet those needs. Romans 12:13 says, "Share with the Lord's people who are in need. Practice hospitality." Giving is a form of generosity, as is hospitality.

Because I believe God owns my house, and my table, I am quite certain that I need to be open to God's purposes for the house, the table, the food I put on it. The added bonus is that when I am generous, I experience joy. Generosity draws me into community, into connection with others and with God.

God gave me the ability to earn the money I receive. I put words together into sentences. I create written resources. From that I earn money. Amazing, isn't it? All I have is entrusted to me to take care of but not to keep. My treasure's not here, not in these things.

Paying college tuition bills for two kids at the same time tested these theories—shoved them up against the wall, poked and prodded. I wanted to grab, to hoard; it would have been easy to lose the ability to trust. When I've risked generosity, God's always provided in amazing ways. I felt grateful for the opportunity not only to bless others with generosity, but to experience God's provision in tangible ways.

The Old Testament called God's people to tithe—to give the first 10 percent of their harvest, their flocks, and so on—and also to make a rather elaborate set of sacrifices over and above that tithe. It is possible to tithe 10 percent and not practice generosity. Jesus accused the Pharisees of this very thing:

> Woe to you, teachers of the law and Pharisees, you hypocrites! You give a tenth of your spices—mint, dill and cumin. But you have neglected the more important matters of the law—justice, mercy and faithfulness. You should have practiced the latter, without neglecting the former. You blind guides! You strain out a gnat but swallow a camel. (Matt. 23:23–24)

Using hyperbole, Jesus mocks these religious leaders, saying they carefully tithe even the smallest, tiniest thing: spices. He doesn't say, "Don't tithe." He says to align your soul with your religion, embrace both the letter of the law, and its spirit—by practicing justice, mercy, faithfulness.

The early church lived generously. They had all things in common and lived in an interdependent community where none had need because they shared everything. The Old Testament commands the tithe, yet the New Testament calls us to even more radical generosity. Following the example of the early church means sharing way more than 10 percent.

How do we translate for our culture today what the Bible says about generosity? How do we practice giving in a way that creates more space for God in our hearts, our lives, our relationships?

## First Things First

Many teachers suggest that the biblical principle of giving God first fruits is one we ought to follow today. We don't give God the leftovers, we are generous first, giving God the first portion of what God has given us the ability to earn.

My pastor likes to say that when you talk about financial giving, there are two kinds of people: people who think those who give 10 percent or more are crazy, and people who think those who don't do so are crazy not to.

The hard part comes when those two types of folks marry one another. Trust me on this.

It's one thing to say God is important, that you want a close relationship. It's another thing to put God in your budget. If we want to create space for God in our lives, we need to create some space in our budget. When the first check we write (or pay online) when we get paid is our giving, it's a bold, powerful declaration of trust, a defiant refusal to give in to fear or doubt. Not just giving, but giving first, reminds us of our priority. It keeps us from frivolous spending, makes us think twice about what we really need and want.

My pastor teaches the 10-10-80 plan: give 10 percent, save 10 percent, live on the remaining 80 percent, adjusting your lifestyle to avoid debt by living within your means. That may seem radical, too. "How would we survive?" you might wonder. Plenty of people make 20 percent less than you, and they survive, right? Generosity requires not just giving, but choosing: what you will buy, drive, live in. These choices impact what you can afford and how generous you are free to be.

I grew up in a family that valued generosity. When I got my first job, my dad, who had been talking to me about money since I was about five years old, talked to me about the value of giving. I don't remember his exact words, but the gist of it was something like "It's your money, you've earned it, so you can decide what to do with it. But you should know that your mom and I have always tithed, and God has blessed us. I recommend that you be generous, and I believe that God will be generous back."

I believed him. But not just because of the stuff we had, the house we lived in. It was more because of the vibe. Some people seemed like they were always striving, always wanting more and more. That was not us. The unspoken understanding at our house was that we lived simply but we had more than enough. We were not fancy people. We were "tuna casserole and church is our social life" types. Still, I had an abundance mind-set, not a scarcity mind-set. Those who have more stuff or more money do not necessarily enjoy an abundance mind-set. Many affluent people I've known have a scarcity mentality that keeps them from enjoying the good things they have.

Generosity was a lifestyle for my parents. My dad's business success, which he credited to God's generosity, allowed us to live comfortably, but also to give generously. We lived below our means. My parents were thrifty but not stingy. Our family vacations were mostly camping trips, often with a group of other families from our church. I watched the way both my parents chose to be generous. They developed relationships with people in ministry and supported them. They opened our home to my youth group on a regular basis.

Many of the kids I went to high school with were affluent. While I didn't consider us rich, I concluded that we must have had an abundance, because we had enough to give away.

What I came to realize is that "enough" is a state of mind. It's less about how much you have and more about how you see what you have. If you fear you don't have enough, the best thing to do is give some of it away. When you're generous, it breaks the grip of fear on your heart. When you give away money, it loses its power over you. You're set free from its power, from the scarcity mind-set. You tell yourself, well, I must have enough, since I am able to give some away and survive.

Whatever you have, if you give some away, becomes more than enough. You begin to see the world through the lenses of abundance, which are only available to those who are brave enough to be generous.

## Giving Quietly

Jesus, talking about money and generosity, taught,

> Be careful not to practice your righteousness in front of others to be seen by them. If you do, you will have no reward from your Father in heaven.
>
> So when you give to the needy, do not announce it with trumpets, as the hypocrites do in the synagogues and on the streets, to be honored by others. Truly I tell you, they have received their reward in full. But when you give to the needy, do not let your left hand know what your right hand is doing, so that your giving may be in secret. Then your Father, who sees what is done in secret, will reward you. (Matt. 6:1–4)

Without revealing what God has told us to keep secret, I will say only this: Giving in secret is incredibly fun. Often, the gift comes just in time, or in just the right amount, to meet a real need and to boost the recipients' faith. The times I have given anonymously are the ones I remember as being most intimate with God.

There's a rush, an indescribable satisfaction mixed with a breathless giddiness at the idea that God would use your hands to touch someone, your resources to communicate love. It may seem scary to give away money, but this is a path to intimacy with God.

That closeness comes when you respond to opportunities to be generous in unconventional, and sometimes inconvenient, ways. When you give in this way, you feel like you're in on some secret with God, especially when you give anonymously. When you hear of a need, and God prompts you to meet it— you'll experience something many people miss.

God's love for you will not change if you say no to this opportunity. Because nothing can change God's love for us. However, our ability to experience that love, our feeling of connection to that love, can be strengthened, enhanced, grown—if we are willing to risk responding to invitations to give.

Such giving deepens connection with God. It reminds us that God is a protector and provider. The times I've been the conduit for God's provision, I felt more assured of God's provision for *me*.

Notice that Jesus says "when you give," not "*if* you give." Generosity is a spiritual practice that is part of following Jesus. Giving is one of those inconvenient ways we build intimacy with God. It's not optional. To trust Jesus with our eternity but not with our resources doesn't make sense.

What's your next step when it comes to generosity? Who could you help anonymously? What might happen if you asked God to guide you in this, asked for specific direction? What if you just went through your ordinary day listening for whispers, for guidance, when it came to generosity—not just with your finances but with your time, with grace?

## Being Generous with Your Life

As I mentioned at the beginning of the chapter, my husband's parents are getting older. Their health issues and our watching out for them is, not unexpectedly, causing some family stress. Each of the four siblings has a different perspective on their parents' challenges and what needs to be done to help them. It's especially difficult for Scot's younger sister, Judy, who lives in Texas and has a demanding career that requires her to travel.

Adding to the "sandwich generation" feel for Judy is the fact that she married late in life, and she and her partner, Brittany, had a baby less than a year ago. Anyone who's reached the stage where their parents are getting older knows that this adds a layer of stress to our already hectic lives. It just gets complicated.

I felt a nudge: love with action. Brittany is experiencing plenty of her own stress while home alone with an eight-month-old, who is crawling, teething, and getting into everything. They live on a country road in a neighborhood with no sidewalks or parks. She has to drive fifteen minutes just to take him to a playground. Brittany's family is in another state. She's trying to build a support network from the ground up. Very few of their friends have kids. They don't attend church, so they don't have that network. Other moms who meet Brittany are friendly, but she's not in a neighborhood where connections can happen easily. Like any new mom, she was overwhelmed and felt isolated.

As we talked with Judy about what's going on with her parents and her job, I thought—this has got to be hard for Brittany. I knew she felt isolated and frustrated. Judy mentioned that she had three business trips in the next month or so, and she felt guilty about being away from Brittany and Liam, but could not opt out of the business trips.

An idea popped into my brain. "Go visit Brittany and the baby." Wait, what? Really? Brittany's quite a bit younger than me, though we get along great. We joke that we are "sister outlaws" instead of sister-in-laws, since we both married into the family. Scot and I and our kids (who were teenagers at the time) attended Brit and Judy's wedding four years ago, and last year, I went down to Texas for the baby shower.

I have Christian friends who wouldn't attend a gay wedding or baby shower. I don't understand them. Jesus calls us to love everyone. My husband's parents didn't come to the wedding (though his mom, to her credit, did come down for the baby shower).

I'd met my darling nephew last summer, when Judy and Brittany visited the family at the lake. During one of many family meetings with his parents about their declining health, Brit and I and Scot's brother's wife left the house.

We pushed Liam in his stroller down the road to the local tavern (more accurately, it's a biker bar), where we drank Blue Moon beers from mason jars on the patio overlooking the lake (Liam, for the record, had a bottle of formula, not beer). It's where we coined the term "sister outlaws," since it's always been clear that although we are in this family by marriage, we're not included in family meetings about touchy subjects. That afternoon, we were deeply grateful that we were excused from that responsibility. We had preferred sitting outside on a beautiful summer day, drinking beer and taking videos of little Liam with our phones, Instagramming mason jars and a baby bottle, having a great conversation.

I have a good relationship with Brit. But she lives in Texas; we don't see each other often. I wondered if this visit idea was a God whisper or a dumb idea. God, you want me to invite myself to her house to hang out?

I texted and asked how she was doing. She immediately answered; she was trying to get out and meet people; she was doing a little better than before, confiding both effort and struggle. Encouraged by the fact that she didn't just text back "Fine," I plunged ahead.

"So this may sound crazy...," I texted. I offered to come down to visit. I told her I was working on a book and kind of wanted to do a little writing getaway, but why not combine it with some time with her?

"YES YES YES" popped onto my screen almost immediately, followed three seconds later by "THAT IS AN AMAZING IDEA" and a few enthusiastic emojis.

Maybe that idea had come from God. God invites us to be generous, not just with our money, but with our lives. Sometimes the requests seem inconvenient. They disrupt, sometimes a little, sometimes a lot. Sure, it will be fun to hang out with Brit—and to play with my little nephew. But do I really think I'll get much writing done? I don't know. I'm trusting that God will provide and bless this step of faith. Did I mention this was a month and a half before my book deadline?

I went online to book a ticket. As if I needed more confirmation that this was a good idea, I found a cheap fare. $81. Round trip, Chicago to Austin. "Okay, God, now you're just showing off," I said.

God invites us to be generous. And God will be generous in return. (Eighty-one dollars round trip?) Do the inconvenient, generous things, and you'll move toward deeper intimacy with God, and with people. Err on the side of love, and you will find yourself experiencing connection. Your spirit will be formed to be more like Jesus, molded into a shape that resembles love. Demonstrate love, even when it is slightly inconvenient, and you may just experience love in a new way. Become a conduit of God's generous love. How else is God supposed to love people except through other people?

If I can embrace the inconvenience of generosity toward my sisters-in-law, I get to experience intimacy with God. And I get a chance to enjoy friendship, connection, fun. The visit reminded me of how much I enjoy spending time with Judy and Brit, what amazing people they are. I get to do something that will not only allow God to love others through me, but will deepen my intimacy with God, and bless me with stronger friendships with my sisters.

## What Is God Inviting You Into?

Maybe you have some anxiety about money. If you're not sure, ask your spouse—they can often see things you can't (I know, annoying). It might be something you didn't grow up with, and it seems illogical to give away money. All I can say is what my dad said: when you're generous, God blesses you. I'm not going all Joel Osteen or prosperity gospel on you—I don't think we can manipulate God into giving us more money if we give some of our money away. But I think God blesses in other ways.

Is giving of your time or money a regular practice right now? If not, what is God inviting you into? If generosity as a practice scares you, take a little time to think about why.

What, specifically, makes you nervous? Write it down, pray it through. Ask for courage to be generous. Test God and see. Dare to actually do what Jesus asks:

> Give, and it will be given to you. A good measure, pressed down, shaken together and running over, will be poured into your lap. For with the measure you use, it will be measured to you. (Luke 6:38)

Imagine that actually happened: a good measure, shaken together and running over, poured into your lap. It's a beautiful image of abundance. When we are generous, God responds with abundance. And we can't help but experience gratitude. Generosity makes room for gratitude, and gratitude inspires us to be generous. It's a beautiful cycle, an upward spiral. How does that work? That's what we'll discuss in the next chapter.

# Gratitude

## Space in My Relationships

Thanksgiving is my favorite holiday. Unlike Easter or Ramadan or Hanukkah, it is not specifically tied to a faith tradition. It invites everyone, with or without faith, to be a little spiritual and practice gratitude. No one asks, "What is the real meaning of Thanksgiving?" because thanksgiving is also an action. Thanksgiving is giving thanks. It's active; you do it. While our culture has created some traditions around it—turkey, mashed potatoes, football, hanging out with relatives whom you may not even like that much—the focus of the holiday is still giving thanks. Recent calls to remove bias from our history (um, the Pilgrims were not always very kind to the Native Americans) don't change the truth: Thanksgiving as a day, at its heart, is about gratitude.

Thanksgiving reflects values shared by many faiths, including Judaism and Christianity: "Give thanks to the LORD, for he is good; his love endures forever" (Ps. 118:1, also Ps. 107:1, and several times in each psalm).

Christmas has been commercialized and politicized; happily, nobody argues about whether we should say "Happy

Thanksgiving." Even people who don't believe in God celebrate Thanksgiving and express gratitude, if not to a higher
power, to the people around them. The commercialism
machine is trying to encroach on this day to be thankful by
opening its stores early, but I resist that. I refuse to shop on
Black Friday (I'm all #optoutside instead), and I absolutely
never shop on Thanksgiving.

Thanksgiving is about gratitude—even when it's hard.
When your family squabbles, or when you're sad because someone who once sat at your table isn't there this year—for any
number of reasons, it's still a day to express thanks, to remember the goodness of God. And when it is hard, as holidays can
be, when you feel sad or lonely, it is a day to *choose* gratitude,
to lean into those realities and say, "Thank you, Lord" in spite
of the circumstances. Sift through life's debris and what weighs
you down, and find the gems. Thanksgiving rolls together
many of the practices in this book: hospitality, worship, generosity, gratitude. Because of the traditions around the table, the
fact that we feast and rest, it feels like a Sabbath.

Confession: at Thanksgiving, I need to lean into the practice of simplicity, because my greatest temptation is to overdo
things. Brine the turkey, make everything from scratch, use
chargers under the plates—a mostly ornamental addition that
never graces my table except at the holidays. But it looks so
fancy, I convince myself they are necessary. However, I digress.
Thanksgiving is one of the few times of year I go on Pinterest. I have a stack of food magazines with turkeys on the cover
that I save and look through each year, having earnest debates
with myself about what to cook and how to cook it. I love
planning the menu, cooking, creating a beautiful table. I have

to remind myself this is not about the fancy meal; this is creating a space for gratitude, for hospitality. I make myself spend time not just planning the menu but thinking about how to get conversation to a deeper place with a group of folks who may not want to go there.

What I want to focus on, and what people remember, is the gratitude. They may have favorite dishes, but no one builds memories around stuffing or mashed potatoes. It's the conversations that matter, that are remembered.

One year, we used smooth river rocks as placeholders. We wrote each person's name on a stone, set in front of their plate. Between dinner and dessert, we read the story in 1 Samuel 7 about Israel's battles against an army far stronger than they, and God's miraculous help, and Samuel setting up a stone altar and calling it Ebenezer ("stone of help") because "thus far has the Lord helped us." Each person wrote a word on their stone, a word that described their year or somehow captured it. One by one, they shared their words, told the story about how God had helped them thus far in the year that was drawing to a close. Together, we built a little altar of Ebenezer stones (and stories) in the middle of the table.

My niece's boyfriend, new to our table that year, told us a story about building a wooden canoe with his father, which was as much about the miracle of relationship as it was about the unusual project. My niece told me that when she spoke to him a few days afterward about what happened at the table, he had tears in his eyes. Why? I asked. Because he felt so loved when we listened to his story, she said. He was a stranger and we welcomed him. To me, it does not get better than that. When I am tempted to spend far too much time focusing on place settings and my collection of November *Bon Appétit* issues, I hold the picture of that conversation in my mind.

We almost always have an eclectic mix of people at our table. That typically includes all or part of my husband's family, but often will include other people we barely know. One November, my husband showed a house to people who were moving into the area from out of state. When he learned they knew no one in the area, he invited them to Thanksgiving dinner at our house. He'd known them two days. I met them when they walked into our house. In the weeks leading up to Thanksgiving, our radar for orphans and strays goes on high alert. We look for opportunities to invite.

One year, we had newly arrived refugees sharing our table. We connected with them through a local relief organization. I remember that year so clearly, explaining the origins of the American holiday (religious persecution led people to seek freedom in a new land) to this Muslim family who'd spent the last ten years in a refugee camp after being displaced by war. They were strangers whose story mirrored the Thanksgiving narrative. We welcomed them, along with another family of friends we've known and loved for years. All our children romped in the backyard, plunked out duets at the piano, shot pool in the basement and hung out together.

In the last few years, we've had as many as we can fit around our dining room table, but then invited others to come for dessert in the evening.

It's November as I write this. We planned to gather with about half of Scot's family, and my friend Sarah, a single mom, and her two boys, and another friend and her elderly mother.

It's quite possible that Scot will find someone else in the meantime who will join us.

Between writing chapters, I've been menu planning, writing up a cooking schedule, shopping for ingredients and place cards, scheming about questions we can ask to get people to express their gratitude (and to steer away from political discussions about the election and the ensuing protests).

Mid-November, my mother-in-law went into the hospital for a scheduled surgery. However, she was too ill to have the surgery, and they admitted her to the hospital for a couple of days, then sent her home. A week before Thanksgiving, we had difficult conversations about her care and next steps, navigating her fears as she faces loss of control over her circumstances. It's hard to feel grateful when you're facing hard family conversations about health care and future plans.

She and my father-in-law made it to our Thanksgiving table, which we shared not only with family but my friend Sarah and her sons and nephews (we met the nephews that day). My mother-in-law eagerly shared her gratitude for good health— she meant she was happy to be well enough to be at the table.

Maybe you're in a season, even if it is not Thanksgiving, where gratitude is hard to muster up, where difficult circumstances make gratitude a stretch. Gratitude feels more than inconvenient; it feels impossible. But when we defiantly choose to be grateful, to be thankful even for the tiny bits of light in a dark life, we experience God in a way that we cannot when everything is sailing along wonderfully. Struggle recalibrates our gratitude, forces it to be more honest, more authentic. We no longer default to that easy prayer, "Thank you for everything" or "Thanks for all you've given us." We're forced to sift through the rubble to find the small, beautiful bits.

This year, as we have hard conversations about my mother-in-law's health, it's keeping me focused on what matters. And guess what? It's not the place settings.

Thanksgiving is rich with traditions, but I never want to become a slave to traditions. My nephews always request that I make my special green beans (which, by the way, do not involve cream of mushroom soup). But I always try to add something new to the menu. I also try to figure out a fresh way to invite people into the practice of gratitude, sometimes with the traditional "What are you thankful for?" but other times with something that brings a new flavor or nuance to the discussion.

Practicing gratitude can fall into predictable patterns. How do I embrace inconvenience when it comes to gratitude? Maybe by being willing to be thankful in the midst of hard things, even being thankful *for* the hard things. Life's challenges need not keep us from practicing gratitude; they can be transformed by our gratitude, from pain to opportunity.

## More Than Counting Blessings

In her best-selling book *One Thousand Gifts*, Ann Voskamp writes of her response to a challenge: list one thousand blessings—things she is grateful for. Ann writes in a beautiful and unique way about the challenge of cultivating gratitude, about keeping a journal in which she poetically begins to list things she's grateful for—the one thousand gifts she discovers are right in front of her. She's talented—anyone who could make life on a pig farm with six children sound so lovely, and find spiritual insights in a soap bubble, has serious writing chops. She's smart, yet relatable, weaving her study of Greek words (*eucharisteo*, to give thanks) into a simple and beautiful description of domestic chores. I don't disagree with a word of what she wrote. Her insights about how blessing comes when we choose to be grateful—profound.

The conclusion she draws from the exercise of simply noticing and writing down things that bring her joy is the mysterious connection between awareness and experience. By taking time to say thanks, she finds she has not only enough blessings but more than enough time to relish them:

> Jesus embraces His not enough....*He gives thanks....*And there is more than enough. *More than enough! Eucharisteo* always, always precedes the miracle. And who doesn't need a miracle like that every day? *Thanksgiving makes time.* Really? Give thanks and get time? Give thanks... slow time down with all your attention—and your basket of not-enough-time multiplies into more than enough time....Thanksgiving creates abundance; and the miracle of multiplying happens when I give thanks."[1]

Our thanksgiving, our giving thanks, our gratitude, creates a God space in our lives and makes room for miracles. It slows us down to God's pace, and gives us more time.

Voskamp's book probably inspired a lot of people to start keeping gratitude journals. Which is a great practice. We do need gratitude in our daily lives, and the practice of putting pen to paper can be transformative. But gratitude must go beyond counting our blessings. As Voskamp learned, the joy and blessing come when we are grateful in spite of our struggles. In fact, *eucharisteo*, giving thanks, can transform our struggles—not erase them, but turn them into something that forms and shapes us into people who are more like Jesus, more compassionate, more tender, more willing to love.

This is not merely positive thinking. Gratitude is not necessarily all about us. It is a discipline that can allow us to experience God in a new way. When we are grateful and give thanks, we experience grace. And that grace flows from us to the people around it who are hungry to taste more of God. They might just encounter grace through us, through our transformation.

I often write my prayers in a journal. Sometimes, these prayers sound like angry comments on a blog or letters to God's complaint department. Ann Voskamp I am not. I spill my thoughts on the page, then try to summarize in a list, under the heading "Help!" or sometimes, "Help?" as in, "A little help here?" I write the names of people I'm praying for, situations I'm struggling with, or what I'm scared or worried about. Isn't it astonishing that we can approach the throne of grace with such confidence and candor?

Once I get that stuff out of the way, I turn to gratitude and make a list. It helps, to assess realistically the good, the strengths, the blessings. But my motive is often self-focused. I mistakenly think that I need to have an "attitude of gratitude" because of what it will do for me—lift my spirits, make me happy, ease my pain.

If you were to open your gratitude journal, should you happen to keep one, and read us a page or two, the things you're most grateful for probably aren't *things*. I don't know about you, but the grateful side of my prayer ledger is mostly names of people and situations where God has somehow orchestrated a result I'm thankful for: a writing gig coming through, conflict resolved, forgiven sin, unexpected grace, reconciliation between two friends I've been praying for, my kids—always my kids. I'm thankful for the opportunity to know and raise them, even as I daily ask for help with that continuing assignment.

## Not Alone

Gratitude is a relational practice. We're grateful for people, or grateful for situations that, inevitably, include and are about people. The relationship central to gratitude is the one we have with God. I'm learning that gratitude is more about the Giver. It's not about me.

If I give someone a gift, their appreciation is, in itself, a gift right back. I'm pleased when people say thank you, when they tell me how my gift blessed them. You probably feel the same way.

I believe that God, like us, is blessed by our gratitude.

We pray individual prayers of gratitude, but gratitude can also be a discipline that we practice in community. We can thank God together and thank one another. Notice the kindness another person has extended to you, especially those you tend to take for granted, like your family. Name and appreciate it; that builds connections. It melts tension that might be lurking. We all want to be appreciated, to know we matter. When we're kind to someone, we want them to at least notice it.

When we practice gratitude, it not only transforms our relationship with God, but it transforms us and changes our relationships with other people. We experience more joy and become more of a joy to be around. Our positive energy pulls other people in, invites them to practice gratitude.

Sometimes, gratitude just wells up, but for me it's usually a discipline. I have to drag myself to the gratitude place and muster some up. There, transformation happens. It's almost like going to the gym or for a run. You have to make yourself do it but when you do, good things happen.

## Nice Pace!

I have wasted a lot of my time, and the time of sympathetic friends, complaining about small problems that felt big. I've tangled myself in the challenges I face, talking them through so thoroughly that I couldn't extricate myself. Even my prayers would be full of complaint and frustration in certain seasons of my life. It just felt so hard. Right now, I'm not feeling grateful because, due to an injury, I can't run. It's bumming me out. (If you don't like to exercise, this might not seem like a downer.) I've been bike riding and even swimming, neither of which is my favorite. I can go to the gym, and walk, although sometimes even walking hurts my knee.

Last year, running was my solace. I'd previously been a recreational and noncommittal runner, but I began training in earnest, and ran ten races, including three half marathons. I was astonished to discover that this training enabled me to do ten-mile runs, to see them as normal.

And then I tweaked my knee. It seemed small. In hindsight, I overestimated my abilities while ignoring my age and fitness level. But it's sidelined me for a few months, and I'm bummed about it. Running kept me going, eased my stress when life was hard or disappointing. The summer my second child left home to go to college, my dog passed away, and a job I enjoyed ended. I struggled. I would get up, but then lie on the couch and feel sad.

Running gave me an outlet, helped me cope, sometimes got me up in the morning. The endorphins the body manufactures when you run long distance seemed to be just the little jolt I needed to function. I joined a running group that gave me a delightful sense of community. I got jazzed by setting new goals and reaching them. I was proud, I admit, to be over fifty and run with little or no pain. I felt strong, happy, invincible. I steadily improved my fitness, speed, endurance.

Now I'm hobbling. Slowly, I am working back to being able to run short distances, but I'm so frustrated. I dislike limits. I have always been a "work hard and get it done" girl who thrives on accomplishment and achievement. Accepting limitations is hard for me.

Gratitude is a discipline. I know this. I realize that I don't need it only when I'm feeling strong and capable. I need it most when I feel hindered, impatient, inadequate. I choose to be thankful, to see the gifts. I appreciate that biking is still an option. This discipline of gratitude is as much work as a long run on a cold day.

On a bike ride the other day, I tried to tell myself that at least I can ride along trails of wildflowers, enjoying the breeze, coasting down hills. I can be outdoors, I can move, I can exercise, just not the way I'd prefer.

Running becomes a part of your identity. I'm not just a person who runs, I'm a runner. The shift, from verb to noun, is hard to explain.

I'm trying to be grateful, to practice gratitude. But it's hard.

I know I was running away from depression and sadness. This stage of life is hard. My kids live two thousand miles away. Life is quiet and, at times, a little dull. I'm working on my marriage after years of focusing mostly on the kids, but that is sometimes hard, too. (The first few months after my youngest went off to college were excruciating.)

Running met my need for adventure. I am a trail runner, the more technical the better. It's hard to find those kinds of trails in Chicago, but I seek them out, and I always enjoy my visits to California where trails are narrow, hilly, and fun.

But I know I was running from pain that an empty (oops, "spacious") nest brought to the light.

Ironically, as I struggle with an injury that slowed me down, I am working on a book about slowing down to "God's pace."

In my running community, we all know each other's pace. Runners talk about pace: race pace, training pace, "are you running at a nine minutes per mile" pace, or "pushing for an 8:30" pace. I wear a watch that shows my running pace, but I can feel my pace without the watch. I've learned this counterintuitive fact: if you do long practice runs at a slow pace, you'll build an endurance that will actually allow you to run faster in races. The most fit in our group can run for miles at a seven minutes per mile pace, a speed I have experienced only when sprinting downhill for about thirty seconds at a time.

We follow each other on a social media app for exercise. One thing we're always looking at: how far and how fast. We post our times for races, especially when we achieve a PR, a personal record. It's a strange and beautiful world, but we talk about pace a lot, mostly in the context of how to run faster. When we post race results, we'll comment to one another, "Nice pace!" Here I am, writing about pace, in a season when mine has slowed considerably.

Is God trying to teach me something? Maybe I need to not be so focused on my running pace, and think instead about the pace of my life. Maybe running so hard, in my life and my work, was wearing not just on my knee but on my soul.

Last night some of my runner friends came over. They offered sympathy, exercises to help my injury, the number of a good chiropractor, advice on why taping is better than wearing a brace, and so on. We talked about fueling and speed work and how and when to stretch. And we talked about this idea of pace, not just in running but in our lives.

My friend Tony, who runs ultramarathons, shared what he wrote about a tough race he ran, in which he questioned why he even runs at all. What's the point? When pain made him walk, he asked a piercing question, "What am I running from?" All of us run from our pain. A few of us do so by literally running. Maybe you do it with food, or wine, or shopping, or being super busy and productive. I've done all of those. Welcome to the club of running away from things.

When you slow down and take a few moments to let gratitude

replace guilt or to let shalom replace shame, you realize that you don't need to run away. Jesus is right there, loving you in the midst of the mess. He sees what you are running from; he wants to heal, forgive, and give you a lighter, easier burden. He invites you to walk—not run—with him. He wants to teach you the unforced rhythms of grace. You can't learn them when your head is full of painful memories, when you're running away from the pain to prove by your accomplishments that you're worthy, that you have significance.

You need prove nothing to the world, and certainly nothing to God. You need only gratitude.

## When You're Not Feeling It

As I was working on this chapter, we had a national election. To say I was disappointed with the results is an understatement. It went far beyond the fact that my preferred candidate lost. The divisiveness made me despair. The wave of racism and sexism and bullying that the election unleashed made me feel sick. Knowing that many of my fellow Christians had helped put a candidate who seemed so unqualified into office made me angry and sad.

The election made me ask myself, again: How do I practice gratitude when life disappoints? How do I praise God when I am so filled with what I consider to be righteous indignation?

In the days following the election, I read news stories and social media and wept. I heard about bullying, watched videos of white supremacists celebrating, and I despaired. I did not feel grateful at all. I wrote publically about the election, about my disappointment, calling people to reach out to the marginalized who were feeling fear in its wake. A couple of well-meaning Christian friends chastised me for stirring things up, accused me of divisiveness. This made me sad, and angry.

The election was having intense consequences for immigrants, people of color, LGBTs. In the first few days after the election, kids were bullied in schools, people were harassed by police, and peaceful demonstrators were assaulted. I felt betrayed by people from my own faith tradition who appeared to have not thought through exactly what would happen as a result of their votes.

Trying to make a list of things that give me joy in the face of the election felt laughable. I often process my thoughts by writing, letting the words spill and swirl until the thoughts begin to flow clear. But most of the words I wrote following the election were scolding, angry. I fancied myself the Old Testament prophet, calling people to repentance. That was not very satisfying. Nor was it helpful. I had to repeatedly walk away from social media, like an addict who keeps on quitting their drug of choice.

I was chatting via text with a friend who'd taken my side in an online argument, when she told me she was going to take a break from the stressful online conversations and go out to the barn and ride her horse. I told her I envied the fact that she had a horse. She invited me to come out and ride with her. And suddenly, a light shone under the door.

I grew up riding. I shoveled manure in exchange for the opportunity to ride for free. I am happiest on the back of a horse. In my junior high years, my horse was the one who listened attentively when I poured out my preteen angst. I've not ridden except on rare occasions for the last twenty-five years, due to kids, life, budget, and so on. But the few times I have, I find it is like riding a bike—you don't forget how. And it's still my happy place.

My grief and frustration over the election could not be staunched with a gratitude list. I needed to engage in physical action, to put myself in the way of joy.

I drove out to the barn the next day. We rode only for a short while, but it was long enough to bring me joy, and that moved me back toward gratitude. It was a step to keep my spiritual life connected to faithful actions (not just thoughts or online comments).

Maybe for you it's gardening or walking on the beach or gazing at the night sky or going for a run or wandering through an art museum. What sparks gratitude for you?

This is not escapism. When despair crowds out gratitude, the discipline of simply giving thanks, of writing down our blessings, can be transformative. Gratitude realigns our souls, reminds us that God is still good. But sometimes, we need more than a list. We need action. We need to get out and do something. Our embodied spirituality is a critical component of gratitude.

What brings you joy? Many of us are so busy taking care of everyone else, at home, work, in our faith community, that we do not know the answer to that question. Your own needs, your own joy, is important. We bring a better self to our workplace, home, faith community, if we are filled with the joy that gratitude emboldens. Joy deepens our connection with God so that we can let love flow through us.

What brings you joy? What do you wish you had more time

for? What would happen to your joy level if you did more of that one thing? Imagine something that you love doing with your physical body, whether it is wandering a botanic garden or running a marathon.

You may be in a stage of life where your time is not your own, where kids or work or aging parents or other people seem to consume your energy and time. I've been there. Ask for help. Carve out an hour a week to do something you enjoy by yourself. Self-care opens us up to gratitude. When we're kind to ourselves, we are empowered to be kind to others.

If you have kids who are too young to be left alone, bring them with you. Invite them into the activities that give you joy. Put them in a stroller and go for a walk. Take them somewhere, get out of the house and into the world, and notice the beauty. Your kids will help you with this if you move at their pace. Stop and admire a bug crossing the sidewalk. Collect fallen leaves. In bleak midwinter, visit a greenhouse and breathe in the smell of life.

When I was growing up, my mom would regularly pack my brother and me into the back seat of our Volkswagen Bug and drive to a forest preserve where we would hike for an hour. Summer, winter, fall, or spring, it didn't matter. We'd #optoutside way before it was a hashtag on a marketing campaign. My brother and I thought it was a great adventure. It was my mom's way of staying sane, coping with being home with two small, rowdy children. In the woods, peace reigned. When I am stressed, I find myself seeking a walk, or a run, in the woods.

Thankfully, I live in an area that has, in between the subdivisions and strip malls, small swaths of forest and trails.

A walk in the woods gets my gratitude flowing in ways merely making a list cannot.

Discover what brings you joy, what causes your gratitude to flow. See it not as an indulgence but a spiritual practice designed to prime the pump of gratitude in your life. Self-care gets us in touch with gratitude; it's essential. Jesus would retreat to the mountains or wilderness, carving out time alone to pray, to replenish his soul.

Soul care differs from self-absorption. We strengthen ourselves in order to reengage with others. The best way to express gratitude for what we have is to share it. That seems counter-intuitive, perhaps, in our grabby consumer culture. If you're grateful for your food, share it. If you're grateful for your home, invite someone into it. If you're grateful for money, use it to bless others. The paradox of gratitude is if we hoard what we are grateful for, our gratitude turns to fear and an insatiable appetite for more. We're impoverished by our greed. When we share what we are grateful for, God blesses it and we enjoy it more.

## Gratitude Collects

Gratitude throws our arms open wide, lifts our downcast faces to see and embrace all the good that God has invited us into. Gratitude collects other practices together, enriching and strengthening them. And those practices, in turn, enhance our gratitude, help us to live grateful and aware. This interweaving transforms us and draws us into intimacy with God in a way that no single practice can.

Listing blessings will raise our awareness of them, but the

power of gratitude is multiplied by connecting it with the other practices that we've been exploring in this book.

Gratitude is a practice that leads us into joy. Joy is not absence of conflict nor merely feeling happy. It is an inner strength and peace we feel in spite of our circumstances, not because of them. Each practice in this book can usher us into gratitude, boosting our joy. Gratitude ties them all together, collecting them in a way that draws us into intimate connection with God.

# Critical Thinking

## Space for Faith and Doubt

In his book *Faith and Doubt*, John Ortberg writes that the word in the middle may be the most important in that phrase. Faith and doubt coexist and actually depend on each other. You cannot doubt nothing. Doubt needs something to push against, and that something is faith.

Ortberg writes,

> Because old Mother Nature is a dysfunctional parent who keeps sending us mixed messages, we need both faith and doubt. The birth of every infant whispers of a God who loves stories; the death of every infant calls his existence into question. Writer Michael Novak says that doubt is not so much a dividing line that separates people into different camps as it is a razor's edge that runs through every soul.... The reality is, we all have believing and doubting inside us. For "we all have the same contradictory information to work with."[1]

The problem comes not when we doubt, but when we are told we are not allowed to do so—even if the one telling us not to doubt is ourselves. Doubt is not rejecting faith, but an invitation to refine it. Maybe you grew up thinking doubt was the ultimate sin, and questioning was rebelling, or worse.

When facing doubts and questions, we need to be merciful to ourselves. The book of Jude, one of the shortest in the Bible, is full of judgment and calling out sin. But then it adds this sweet little thought: "Be merciful to those who doubt" (v. 22). Sometimes, I think, the hardest skeptic to show mercy to is yourself.

I'm at the stage of my life where many of my friends are sending their kids off to college and panicking. They're realizing that if the kids haven't questioned their faith yet, they probably will in college, where they're going to be exposed to a variety of worldviews, many of them very different from their own. The idea of their kids leaving the bubble can make them feel scared, so they use words like *rebellion* and *prodigal* and *losing their faith* a lot.

If you teach your children only *what* to think, but never teach them *how* to think, you'll end up with either rebels or robots. They'll never have the chance to develop their own faith. Even if you send them to a private school to keep them in the bubble for another four years, eventually they have to get out in the world where people will think differently. Their faith will never be their own if they don't get a chance to test it, strengthen it by questioning, or hold it up to the weight of doubt and come out the other side with a stronger faith.

This is why critical thinking is such an essential spiritual practice. Belief is not just about faith but about ideas.

We all need a muscular faith—strong, wiry, capable of

engaging with ideas and sorting fact from fiction. We need to develop discernment. In order to do that, we've got to face our doubts and questions. In a world where lying and spin have become so normal, the ability to think critically is especially essential, not just for our spiritual lives but for our civic and political lives as well.

As the wisest man in the ancient world observed: "The gullible believe anything they're told; the prudent sift and weigh every word" (Prov. 14:15 MESSAGE). "Sift and weigh every word" is a pretty good definition of critical thinking, and the Bible recommends it.

## Strengthening Yourself

Physical exercise operates on a paradox: In order to strengthen a muscle, you must break it down. To build lung capacity, you must push to the limits, getting "out of breath" for a short time. To improve your endurance, you have to push yourself past your current capacity.

My friend Christine, who owns the indie coffee shop where my running group often gathers after our Saturday morning runs, is training to audition for *American Ninja Warrior*. I've watched her transform her body into compact, solid muscle. Even when she fell and blew out her knee, she didn't give up. She worked through the rehab and kept going. I'm in awe of her determination and what she's become able to do.

As mentioned before, I challenged myself to take my occasional maintenance running to the next level. Although I'm in my early fifties, I gradually increased my strength and endurance enough to run several half marathons. By pushing myself to run farther, I became *able* to run farther.

The same is true for faith. By pushing against our doubts, wrestling with the questions, we develop a sturdy, resilient faith that can handle dispute, argument, debate, and uncertainty. If I am willing to embrace the paradox that in order to build strength I must push my muscles to the point of weakness, I should be willing to see the parallels that lie in the relationship between faith and doubt.

My favorite seventeenth-century poet, John Donne, wrote, "To come to a doubt, and to a debatement of any religious duty, is the voice of God in our conscience: Would you know the truth? Doubt, and then you will inquire." Donne's point: Doubt is actually God's voice, asking us to test, asking us to inquire about truth. Inviting us with a winsome smile, "Seek, and you will find."

In response to Donne's observation, Madeleine L'Engle writes, "If my religion is true, it will stand up to all my questioning; there is no need to fear. But if it is not true, if it is man imposing strictures on God...then I want to be open to God, not to what man says about God."[2]

Rainer Maria Rilke said, "Live the questions." Perhaps someday, you'll find an answer, or you'll realize that the daily asking, the periodic doubts, are themselves the answer. The questions and doubts are what constitute a life of faith.

We often hold up examples who seem to have unshakable faith, who never seem to doubt. However, faith heroes like Mother Teresa and the apostle Paul wrestled with doubt. Jesus, when he encountered doubters, did not walk away, but encouraged them to see that doubt is the flip side of faith. Doubt, it gets a bad rap. Galileo doubted that the sun revolved around the earth. His "heresy" got him in big trouble (he was excommunicated and spent the rest of his life under house arrest), but his doubt ultimately led to truth. Doubt facilitates faith. If we are willing to engage with confrontations to our faith, that faith will be strengthened. Your deepest doubt may be God's voice in your conscience.

## What Do You Think?

When my kids were small and came to me with a problem, I'd listen carefully, and say, "Well, what do you think?" I tried not to solve their problem for them. Oftentimes, the "problem" was "I'm bored!" and my answer was "It sounds like you have a problem. But you are a smart and capable person, so I think you can solve your own problem."

Setting healthy boundaries with kids means not making their problems my problem. I was not going to solve their boredom problem, because that's not my job as a parent. My job was to raise capable, autonomous people who can solve their own problems, or at least not expect other people to fix their problems.

If they couldn't figure out how to entertain themselves, I did offer to alleviate my children's boredom by assigning chores. And I was always glad to listen if they wanted to talk about how to solve their problems.

As they got older, I gave them the same response when they faced conflicts with friends, dilemmas over scheduling, and even doubts about their faith. We encouraged them to be curious, to ask questions, to read and problem-solve. In other words, to think critically. I tried to listen and ask good questions, although I sometimes failed (my kids will tell you that).

When my kids hit their teens they began to question the faith tradition we'd raised them in. They still went to church but let me know that they weren't sure they believed, that they had questions.

I told them their feelings were okay with me. God could handle their doubts and questions. I said it was necessary to question, because it would strengthen their faith. Going to church would give them something to think about, to question. Reading theology, listening to messages, would give them specific ideas to wrestle with.

My daughter attended a Christian college that also encouraged students to fearlessly speak their doubts and questions. For some, it was a new experience. Melanie thanked me for letting her ask those questions way before she got to college.

When she was seventeen, she asked us about the differences between religions. She was specifically curious about Islam, and what the Qur'an said. I admitted I'd never read it. Scot had a Muslim coworker and friend, and so he asked that friend if he'd be willing to loan Melanie his copy of the Qur'an to read. So, for a season in high school, Melanie's nightstand held three books: the Qur'an, the Bible, and C. S. Lewis's *Mere Christianity*. She was doing her own comparative study. I wrote about it for a magazine and included this observation:

She lives this truth: Faith and doubt coexist in every human heart. God is big enough to handle the questions, and faith is strengthened by our curiosity and inquiry. When she'd come to me with questions over the last nearly two decades, I'd often start with "Well, what do you think?" We have talked, without labeling them as such, about theology, hermeneutics, interpretation, doctrine. . . .

Especially at this stage of the game, we are trusting our daughter's spiritual and intellectual maturity enough to allow her to read both C. S. Lewis and the Qur'an, to see what truth each contains. By allowing her to read the Qur'an, we said with our actions, "We trust you. And we think Christianity is compelling enough that honest inquiry into what other faiths believe will only strengthen your faith in Jesus."[3]

## Faith Is a Strenuous Journey

I've seen two responses to our increasingly pluralistic, diverse society. Some embrace multiculturalism—an acceptance of various points of view. Others react against it—dig in to dearly held convictions, values, and traditional interpretations.

I stand for values, but that can become dangerous when we hold firm to ideas without careful discernment. Periodically, we must strenuously reexamine our beliefs, to determine if they are right, and whether they're still of value, not only to us but also to the people around us.

Doubt is the dark that enables us to see the light of faith. Most of us both doubt and believe simultaneously, if we're honest. One minute I'm writing and teaching about the life of faith, so thankful and connected with God; the next, I wonder if I'm making it all up. I accept that tension; I live in it; I need it for my faith to mean anything.

Faith without doubt is not really faith. For faith to have meaning, it has to be placed in what could potentially not be true.

We need to love the questions and not be in such a hurry to resolve them. Rilke, a German poet, wrote to a young friend in the early 1900s,

> I beg you... to be patient toward all that is unsolved in your heart and to try to love *the questions themselves* like locked rooms and like books that are written in a very foreign tongue. Do not now seek the answers, which cannot be given you because you would not be able to live them. And the point is, to live everything. *Live* the questions now. Perhaps you will then gradually, without noticing it, live along some distant day into the answer."[4]

We often hear faith described as a journey. The metaphor has less power because few of us ever go on journeys anymore. We hop on a plane, watch a movie, drink a Pepsi, and four hours later we're on the other side of the country. It's not a journey. The closest thing to a journey we experience is the TSA line.

A true journey is hard; it requires effort, problem solving. Roads can be flat and smooth, or uphill, rocky, muddy, or even hard to find. We notice it's sunny or rainy because we are walking, not just sitting.

What type of journey is faith to you? Are you on a cross-country flight, or a strenuous cross-country hike? What would happen if you got curious about God?

On the journey of faith, we encounter obstacles, take detours, even experience crises. We may think these are setting us back, but ultimately they get us closer to God. Our goal is not lack of doubt but depth of intimacy with our Lord. If we apply the discipline of critical thinking to our faith journey, we'll see the value of doubts and ultimately benefit from them.

On our journey of faith, there are four distinct stages, according to Dr. Henry Cloud.[5] Most people, as they go through life, follow a spiritual path that looks a bit like this, according to Cloud:

Stage 1: Non-faith/Self-ruled. Before we discover God, or come to believe, we are our own god, though we may not articulate it that way. We eventually wonder—is there a God, and what do I think about that God? Being our own god usually leads us to a painful place: meaninglessness, or addiction, or broken relationships. Cloud explains that we often end up in a "crisis of meaning" where we wonder, "Is this all there is to life?"

Stage 2: Entering through the door of faith. We find the answers to our "What's life all about?" questions in God. This is a fun and exciting stage, as we are feeling quite certain and grateful that we've found the truth, we affirm that God exists, and loves us. We experience a feeling of coming home, of finding truth we can depend on, and, oftentimes, rules we can follow. In this stage, the structure of faith provides security. We're relieved that we aren't on our own and we now have direction and help. Cloud notes that we can easily become legalistic in this stage. We see life as fitting into neat formulas that work in every situation. We try to tell other people to use those formulas, and we have trouble seeing the gray between the black and white answers we think we've found. We learn discipline and rules, Cloud says, but eventually, he notes that "we become intolerable to those in other stages" as we become more rigid and convinced in our thinking.

Many people never get past stage two, or stay there for a very long time. But in stage two, cracks eventually begin to develop. Things don't always fit the formulas. Good people experience difficulties. Tragic things happen. Cancer, divorce, war, pain. They're all part of life—even the lives of faithful people who trust God. Doubts come to mind, unbidden, when we lie awake at night. Confused, we dig in deeper, and try to make the formulas work. Cloud comments, "With our formulas and our missionary zeal, we have become weird and we end up turning off those who are not spiritually open to faith or God, instead of drawing them in." Honestly, I've been weird about things of faith. It's refreshing to have him name it!

When doubts arise, some fear they have lost their faith. They may retreat into shame instead of pushing forward. They haven't learned the discipline of critical thinking; they haven't learned that doubt is part of faith. They're frightened of their doubts, so they either stop talking about them or retreat to legalism, which moves them backward in their journey.

But the brave, who keep going, enter stage three.

**Stage 3:** Pain and Trouble. In this stage, Cloud says people now realize the formulas don't work. This often feels like a crisis of faith, but if we push through it, we find God in the desert. If we face our pain, we realize God is still there with us, not necessarily taking it away but being near and deeply present with us. We find a community of others who have also been in this stage, and we experience God in that community. This is the hard part of the journey, where the path gets treacherous. But if we keep going, we eventually reach the next stage.

**Stage 4:** Worship. In this stage, we don't regain our previous faith, but it matures, as we realize we can't fully comprehend God, and that we don't have all the answers. Formulas and easy answers have been cast off. We embrace mystery. We're humbled, which is what we must be in order to truly worship God. We can live in the tension of faith and doubt, realizing that both coexist in every human heart.

A few years ago, I was invited to speak to a church Bible study and discussion group for mothers of teenagers. I asked my then-seventeen-year-old daughter what I should talk about, what moms of teens needed to know. She told me about Henry Cloud's stages of faith, and said they'd been helpful to her.

I shared these stages with the moms. A number of them

were deeply worried because their teens, especially when they went off to college, seemed to be losing their faith. Their kids were actually journeying through stage three. As they discussed the information I'd given them, it became painfully clear to some of the moms that they were freaking out about their kids because they themselves had never gotten to stage three. They'd been told to believe and not doubt, and they had. These moms had suppressed or ignored their questions instead of exploring them. They didn't realize that moving from stage two to stage three was not backsliding but a step toward maturity.

A lot of us get stuck in stage two because we don't want to rock the boat. We've been conditioned to please people, to not speak up. We confuse critical thinking with being critical. Being negative is not critical thinking. Critical thinking means not just accepting answers but discerning by using the mind God gave you to seek deeper understanding. It means asking good questions.

I encouraged the moms in that room to be brave. What would help their kids best navigate this season was for the moms to do their own spiritual work—ask their own questions, examine their own doubts. This would open them to the opportunity to move out of stage two and into stage three, where the moms could let go of formulas and easy answers, and display authentic faith journeys to their offspring.

We can stay stuck in stage two, afraid or self-medicating to avoid the crisis of faith. Instead of critical thinking, we engage in self-criticism, beating ourselves up for not having more faith. We miss the crisis that inevitably launches us into the desert. We lose an opportunity to find out for ourselves that

God will meet us in the desert. God will walk with us through stage three and into stage four.

I've been in stage three. It's hard. From what I can tell, my twenty-year-old is in this stage right now. Without pushing to know every detail of their interior world, I am encouraging my kids to live the questions. And I continue to live my own questions, to admit when I have doubts. I trust that God is with them on the journey, even when they are not aware of it. I also trust that they've learned the practice of critical thinking enough to apply it to their doubts and their faith. I trust and pray they'll come through this wrestling and questioning season with faith that is stronger. I hope they discover that God is much more than they ever thought.

Certainty is not the destination of the faith journey. It is awe and awareness that there are no easy answers.

The practice of critical thinking ultimately refines and strengthens our faith, though it may not seem to do so at first. It's a practice not just for the big questions of faith but also the daily living of it, particularly when it comes to the practice of reading Scripture.

## Critical Thinking about Scripture

In many Christian traditions, reading the Bible is the most commonly known and practiced spiritual discipline. The one we're "supposed" to do, alongside prayer. It seems fairly straightforward: open and read. It's God's Word. But how do we understand these sacred pages?

How we approach the Bible often mirrors how we navigate

our faith. Dogmatic people will find rules; compassionate people will find mercy; story lovers will be swept away by the truth, grace, and beauty of God revealed. Skeptics may find what seem to be contradictions or oddities.

The Bible is all that and more: rules, justice, mercy, grace, story, and yes, oddities. (Don't believe me? Read Judges 14, for example.)

The Bible offers us a path to intimacy with God, but reading it takes time, discipline, and discernment. That last one is often the hardest to come by.

I love to get up before anyone else and sit on the couch or on the back deck with my coffee, journal, and Bible, and listen. God speaks—through the words on the page, in whispers to my soul, through the beauty of the trees and birdsong, by leading my musings on the pages of my journal. I think and discover by writing, asking questions, occasionally ranting.

As much as I enjoy this practice, I'm wildly inconsistent with it. I've spent decades of my life reading almost every day, and other years where I do it a lot less. I've had seasons where I was writing a Bible study lesson every week, and let that work suffice for my time in Scripture.

Having read the Bible for almost half a century, I assume, at times, I won't learn anything new. I confess that stubborn, prideful attitude. What's amazing? How often a new idea, a fresh thought, comes from even a familiar passage. God does speak through the words on the page.

Taking fifteen minutes or so to read and reflect each day is not that difficult—but many of us find it challenging. People tell me they're afraid they won't understand it, while others have read it and heard it preached so often that it feels too familiar. If, like me, you've led Bible studies or taught classes on the Bible, it gets a little too easy to just skim through and not learn anything new, to be blinded by your pride and familiarity.

In an increasingly dogmatic culture, it's essential to develop discernment—the ability to understand and think critically about what we read. It may be hard to give yourself permission to ask questions or think critically if you were told not to doubt or not to wonder, or if you grew up in a tradition like mine where you heard "God said it, I believe it, that settles it!" Those attitudes were accompanied by interpretations of Scripture that no one dared to disbelieve or even question. So rather than risk misunderstanding or confusion, we skip reading the Bible altogether. Or we just read it to get it done, without questioning it. Or we read and never figure out how to apply it, never asking what it means to us today.

While reading the Bible is an essential practice, I invite you to take it one step beyond mere reading, and practice critical thinking about Scripture. In secular academia, critical thinking refers to the intellectual work of analyzing and evaluating information. Critical thinking seeks to understand information and situations, vigorously fact-checks ideas, and seeks to interpret them with careful reasoning.[6]

In my talk to moms of teenagers, I emphasized the difference between criticizing our faith and thinking critically about it. Blind criticism, however, is no better than thoughtless acceptance. People of faith must engage in critical thinking so that those who don't share our faith can't baselessly criticize. Just because intellectuals question the Bible or a life of faith does *not* mean Christians should be anti-intellectual.

We need to know what we believe and be able to talk about it with reason and insight. The Bible asks us to think critically, not just about Scripture but about our faith and about life.

In his letter to a young church in Thessalonica, the apostle Paul wrote, "Do not scoff at prophecies, but test everything that is said. Hold on to what is good" (1 Thess. 5:20–21 NLT). The Bible itself tells us to think critically, and it is a tool for critical thinking. We get our word *critical* from the Greek *kritikos*, which is only used once in the Bible, to talk about... the Bible:

> For the word of God is alive and active. Sharper than any double-edged sword, it penetrates even to dividing soul and spirit, joints and marrow; it judges [*kritikos*] the thoughts and attitudes of the heart. (Heb. 4:12)

"Unfortunately, 'critical thinking' has sometimes gotten a bad name, especially in very conservative Protestant circles because it is associated with people negatively assessing or even criticizing the Bible. This is unfortunate on various grounds," theologian Dr. Ben Witherington observes. "In the context of conservative Protestantism, there has often been an anti-intellectual spirit that has ruled out of court, ab initio, critical thinking. This has been seen as corrosive or destructive to a person's Christian faith."[7]

Test everything. Think critically. Don't be afraid of your questions and where they might lead you. Hold on to the good, but only after you've tested and questioned and wondered and wrestled.

## Asking Questions Grows Faith

I grew up in a faith tradition with a high view of Scripture. We firmly held to the doctrine of Biblical inerrancy. The Bible had no mistakes, and it was completely true. I was taught that it was basically dictated from God to people, and it was without error in the original languages. Some folks didn't even throw in that caveat about original languages. It was inerrant in the King James Version, as well, in their opinion.

Then I read it for myself. I had some questions. I now believe the Bible is true, with parts a true metaphor, or a true parable. Also, interpretations and translations are not necessarily spot-on. God is infallible, but people are definitely fallible and biased. Understanding the cultural context is absolutely essential for faithful interpretation. The Bible's been misinterpreted and even twisted. Well-meaning, sincere people draw different conclusions when reading the Bible. Christians differ on their interpretation of individual verses and on the overall message of Scripture. When we think that ours is the only correct interpretation, we've lost the ability to think critically.

I was raised to value biblical inerrancy *and* intellectual curiosity. As I continued to grow in my faith, I learned the importance of historical context, figures of speech, and how meanings can get lost in translation from Hebrew or Greek to English, and from thousands of years ago to now. I realized the Bible was a collection of sixty-six books, of a variety of genres: poetry, wisdom and apocalyptic literature, historical narrative, theological treatise, correspondence, and more.

Some parts of Scripture seem to have been written for a specific situation only (No shellfish! No weaving together linen and flax!), while others were universal truths or injunctions (Love your neighbor as yourself!).

Deciding which category verses go into is where the fireworks start. What seems obvious may not be the meaning at all when you look at the historical context and culture. What's clear in an entire passage can appear to mean something entirely different when that passage is wrenched out of context.

Asking questions is a brain workout, and asking spiritual questions is a soul workout. Don't be afraid of questions. As the poet Rilke says, love questions, because of what they will do for you. When we wrestle with our doubts, we grow stronger. The same is true when we are asked hard questions about our faith and perhaps need to admit doubt.

I was halfway through Wheaton, a Christian college, when I became cynical and a bit disillusioned. I transferred to the University of Pennsylvania, an urban, secular, Ivy League university about ten times the size of Wheaton, and in almost every way its opposite. Penn is in south Philly, Wheaton is in an affluent suburb. Penn's enrollment was about 60 percent Jewish, while Wheaton's was 100 percent Christian. (You had to sign a document professing faith to attend.) Penn was home to one of the largest gay student organizations in the country at that time; Wheaton's few gays were very carefully closeted.

At Penn, I eagerly engaged in conversations with incredibly smart people from a wide variety of backgrounds. These conversations forced me to wrestle with my faith, and I found myself defending it. For the first time, I was asked, "How can you call yourself an intellectual and believe in God?"

I'd always heard "How can you call yourself a Christian" questions, but they usually had to do with drinking, dancing, or other activities once forbidden to evangelicals, or something equally wild, like being a Democrat. I wish I were kidding.

But "How can you call yourself an *intellectual*?" That was new. Listening carefully to the questions posed to me by my new friends grew my faith. I had always valued intellectual questioning. I refused to check my mind at the door when pursuing a life of faith. I found the environment at Penn stimulating and exciting. All the "proofs for the existence of God" I'd learned growing up did me little good in discussions with very smart, very cynical people. Citing the Bible as a reference got me laughed at, but it didn't destroy my faith in the Bible. I realized that people accept the Bible as a credible source only when their lives are changed by Jesus. The skeptics might not have read the Bible, but they were reading my life and my words. Did I live what I talked about?

Their questions forced me to examine my faith and test it. They forced me to live according to the truths I argued for. Ultimately, the experience strengthened my faith. Engaging in respectful discussion, listening and learning from their questions, pushed me to think critically, allow faith to exist along with doubt, and live my faith by loving people.

Do you regularly put yourself in situations where you're talking and listening respectfully with people who hold viewpoints different from yours? Do you read a variety of sources for your news and political commentary, not just the ones that support your views? Do you associate and converse with people who vote differently from you, or come from a different faith tradition or culture? Hearing a variety of opinions and perspectives will hone your faith and sharpen it. It will create some space for God to strengthen you both spiritually and intellectually.

## Living in God Space

Critical thinking is most productive when we don't hurry it—when we approach Scripture, or even our daily newsfeed, with care and discernment. We cannot hurry this practice. Slowing down to God's pace when it comes to our thinking means we refuse to let our emotions or instincts hijack our brains.

In the introduction to this book, I invited you to consider living your faith, engaging in an embodied spirituality, a faith lived in the body and in your actions. Spiritual practices are not merely intellectual exercises but what we do in our lives, ways we interact with the world, with others, and with God. But they are in part *intellectual*, and critical thinking is necessary to engage in each one.

In the opening pages of this book, I wrote that God is as close as the air we breathe, and I asked you to open your eyes to begin to see all of your life as lived in the space of God. As this book closes, I hope you will also open your mind to living a new way in God.

Practices of Sabbath, hospitality, worship, simplicity, generosity, gratitude, and critical thinking challenge us to embrace inconvenience. They call us to an embodied spirituality, to live our faith with our hands and feet and calendars and checkbooks, and, yes, minds. Ultimately, the practices bring us into an awareness and intimacy with God that comforts and strengthens our souls. We also find ourselves in more intimate connection with other people. We love and are loved. We extend grace, and receive it back in abundance.

Let your adventure begin with these interconnected practices. Build one on another. Try them, play with them, let them lead you to other practices, new experiences. Slow down to God's pace, open up God space, and embrace the inconvenient adventure of intimacy with God.

# Acknowledgments

Books are birthed out of a writer's experiences, relationships, struggles, and joys. Consequently, no one writes a book alone. Every story that intersects a writer's life, even if not explicitly told in a book, influences it, because those stories shape us. When one writes about faith, the stories and input of every teacher, every mentor, every spiritual friendship, every book, even people one struggles to love, are threads in the tapestry.

Which means, it is impossible to thank everyone who's helped with this book, because I'd have to thank everyone I've ever talked to or every author I've ever read.

However, there are a few people who were directly involved with this project and deserve mention (and much gratitude).

Thank you to my wonderful writing community, Ink Creative Collective. Susy Flory, Caryn Rivadeneira, and Jennifer Grant have each been particularly supportive. Thank you, dear friends, for making writing a less lonely endeavor.

My agent, Steve Laube, convinced me that I had another book to write, and his support and faith is the main reason this book even got written in the first place. Thanks for believing in me.

One of the best parts about writing this book: working

with the team at FaithWords/Hachette. Adrienne Ingrum, my incredible editor, has encouraged, challenged, and stretched me as a writer. And her wonderful assistant, Grace Tweedy Johnson, kept things moving forward and was so patient with me. I'm grateful and honored.

My launch team, led by my dear friend Lynn Siewert, helped me announce with trumpets the arrival of this book into the world. Thank you for all your hard work! And the marketing team at FaithWords—I couldn't have done it without you. Thank you!

Finally, thanks also to my husband, Scot, and my kids, Melanie and Aaron. The adventure of marriage, parenting, and being a family continues to amaze me. All of you have taught me so much as we practiced our faith together.

# Notes

## In Our Crowded Life, Where Does God Fit?

1. Dallas Willard. *The Spirit of the Disciplines*. New York: Harper Collins, 1988, p. 19 (emphasis in the original).
2. Ibid., pp. 29–30 (empasis in the original).
3. Parker Palmer. *Let Your Life Speak*. San Francisco: Jossey-Bass, 2000, p. 3.

## Sabbath: Space in My Calendar

1. Walter Brueggemann. *Sabbath as Resistance*. Louisville, KY: Westminster John Knox Press, 2014, pp. 2–3 (emphases in the original).
2. Ibid., p. 28 (emphases in the original).
3. Ibid., pp. 28–29.
4. G. K. Chesterton once observed: "The Christian ideal has not been tried and found wanting. It has been found difficult; and left untried." (*What's Wrong with the World*. CreateSpace edition, 2014, p. 13.)
5. Mark Buchanan. *The Rest of God*. Nashville, TN: W. Publishing Group, 2006, p. 93.
6. Ibid., p. 129.

## Hospitality: Space in My Home

1. Parker Palmer. *The Company of Strangers*. New York: Crossroad Publishing, 1981, p. 69.
2. At time of publication, this website had helpful info on family meals: "The Big Benefits of Family Meals," North Dakota State University, https://www.ag.ndsu.edu/eatsmart/eat-smart.-play-hard.-magazines-1/2009-eat-smart-play-hard-magazine/test-item.
3. See http://www.biblestudytools.com/dictionary/zarephath/.

4. Ray Vander Laan, *Walking With God in the Desert Discovery Guide*. Grand Rapids, MI: Zondervan, 2010, p. 113.

## Worship: Space in the World

1. John Ortberg. *If You Want to Walk on Water, You've Got to Get Out of the Boat*. Grand Rapids, MI: Zondervan, 2001, p. 195.
2. Jonathan Aigner. "8 Reasons the Worship Industry Is Killing Worship." *Ponder Anew* (blog). Patheos. October 19, 2015. http://www.patheos.com /blogs/ponderanew/2015/10/19/8-reasons-the-worship-industry-is-killing -worship/.
3. For all 107 questions of the so-called shorter catechism, see http://www .opc.org/sc.html.
4. Delesslyn A. Kennebrew. "What Is True Worship?" *Christianity Today*. November 6, 2012. http://www.christianitytoday.com/biblestudies/bible -answers/spirituallife/what-is-true-worship.html?start=1 (emphases in the original).
5. Catherine Clark Kroeger and Mary J. Evans, eds. *The IVP Women's Bible Commentary*. Downers Grove, IL: InterVarsity Press, 2002, p. 640.

## Simplicity: Space in My Soul

1. Richard J. Foster. *The Celebration of Discipline*. New York: Harper & Row, 1988, p. 79 (emphases in the original).
2. Marie Kondo. *The Life-Changing Magic of Tidying Up*. Berkeley, CA: Random House / Ten Speed Press, 2014, pp. 41–42.
3. Richard J. Foster. *Freedom of Simplicity*. New York: HarperCollins, 1981, p. 45.

## Generosity: Space in My Budget

1. Shane Claiborne. *The Irresistible Revolution*. Grand Rapids, MI: Zondervan, 2006, p. 117.

## Gratitude: Space in My Relationships

1. Ann Voskamp. *One Thousand Gifts*. Grand Rapids, MI: Zondervan, 2010, p. 72 (emphasis in the original).

## Critical Thinking: Space for Faith and Doubt

1. John Ortberg. *Faith and Doubt*. Grand Rapids, MI: Zondervan, 2008, p. 23.

2. Madeleine L'Engle. *Walking on Water*. New York: Bantam Books, 1982, p. 134 (originally published by Harold Shaw Publishers in 1980).

3. Keri Wyatt Kent. "Nurturing Faith and Curiosity." *Today's Christian Woman*. January 2013. http://www.todayschristianwoman.com/articles /2013/january/nurturing-faith-and-curiosity.html?start=1.

4. Rainer Maria Rilke. *Letters to a Young Poet*. New York: Modern Library, 2001, pp. 34–35.

5. Dr. Cloud has spoken on this topic in many venues, including Willow Creek Community Church. Watch at https://willowcreek.tv/sermons/south -barrington/2012/08/stages-of-faith/.

6. See the Foundation for Critical Thinking's website at http://criticalthinking .org.

7. Ben Witherington. "Critical Thinking—What Is It and Why Is It Important to Believers?" *The Bible and Culture* (blog). Patheos. April 29, 2012. http://www .patheos.com/blogs/bibleandculture/2012/04/29/critical-thinking-what -is-it-and-why-is-it-important-to-believers/.

# About the Author

Photo by Michael Vanderaa

KERI WYATT KENT is the author of eleven books and coauthor of a dozen others. She is the founder and president of A Powerful Story, which provides writing, editing, and marketing services.

A longtime member of Willow Creek Community Church, she serves there as a lay pastor.

She and her husband, Scot, live in the Chicago area and have two adult children.

Connect with her on social media or at www.keriwyattkent .com.